THE FIRST TWO BOOKS OF POEMS

The First Two Books of Poems

ROBERT PINSKY

WITH A NEW PREFACE
BY THE AUTHOR

PRINCETON UNIVERSITY PRESS
PRINCETON & OXFORD

The original editions of *Sadness And Happiness* and *An Explanation of America* were published by Princeton University Press as part of the Princeton Series of Contemporary Poets.

Some of the poems in this book have originally appeared in the following: *American Poetry Review, American Review, Antaeus, Canto, Chicago Review, Little Square Review, Modern Occasions, The Nation, The New Yorker, New England Review, Ploughshares, PN Review, Poetry, Shenandoah, The Southern Review, Stand, The Yale Review,* and *The Style of the Short Poem.*

Published by Princeton University Press
41 William Street, Princeton, New Jersey 08540
99 Banbury Road, Oxford OX2 6JX
press.princeton.edu

GPSR Authorized Representative: Easy Access System Europe - Mustamäe tee 50, 10621 Tallinn, Estonia, gpsr.requests@easproject.com

All Rights Reserved

ISBN (pbk.) 9780691278230
ISBN (epub) 9780691289793
ISBN (PDF) 9780691278247

Library of Congress Control Number: 2025951474

British Library Cataloging-in-Publication Data is available

Editorial: Erik Beranek
Production Editorial: Theresa Liu
Jacket / Cover Design: Chris Ferrante
Production: Lauren Reese
Publicity: Natalie Zander

Cover image: *Broadway, Long Branch, N.J.,* ca. 1930–1945. Tichnor Brothers Collection. Boston Public Library, Arts Department. Courtesy of Digital Commonwealth.

This book has been composed in Arno

10 9 8 7 6 5 4 3 2 1

CONTENTS

III. PERSONS

IV. THE STREET OF FURTHEST MEMORY

V. ESSAY ON PSYCHIATRISTS

An Explanation of America (1979)

PREFACE

WHEN *Sadness And Happiness* and *An Explanation of America* were first published, in 1975 and 1979, both titles might have seemed aggressively unconventional or "unpoetic." For the first book, two flat abstractions as broad as a child's names for feelings. In the second book's title, the word "*Explanation*" can be read as going defiantly further in the same kind of deadpan, quasi-naive direction.

But defiance and aggression were not what I intended. For me, the titles were comically introspective: a way of teasing myself, more than the reader. The actual writing came first, and I wasn't sure I understood its manners or its weird ambitions.

Where did these books come from?—

Early, rudimentary experience as a performing musician in my teens taught me the joy of theme-and-variation, contrasting regular with irregular, recurrence with surprise. Reaching for improvisation as meaning, the jumpy non sequiturs in these first books stem from that jazz-chorus experience of form, more than any literary poetics.

Of course I also had literary instruction, beginning with the great teaching of Francis Fergusson at Rutgers. Fergusson described Aristotle's *Poetics* as a cookbook for writers, based on the idea of an *action* played out by the "arrangement of the incidents" that is the soul of the tragedy. Plotting the parts of a play into the right order can enact the movement-of-soul in each character, driving every speech as a component vector in the action of every scene and each scene as a component moving part in the overall action of the dramatic entirety—and ultimately a movement-of-soul in the audience. Non sequiturs or digressions or the vagaries of a story all can enact the spiritual clarity of a work's action, as unforeseen yet inevitable as music: we are moved. Like the praxis of a play, I decided, the arc of a poem can embody a movement of the soul. That idea reminded me of a high compliment among jazz musicians: that a performance was "going somewhere."

In a more complicated, even contradictory way, my writing still comes from the repulsive, brilliant, dictatorial, pedantic, infuriating, and illuminating instruction of Ezra Pound. His *ABC of Reading*, a textbook that is also a parody of textbooks, was assigned by Paul Fussell, my teacher in Freshman Composition. Unlike many poets my age, I never had much interest in Pound's episodic, hyper-allusive, fragmentary *Cantos* as an example of the long poem, still less in his theories of economics or government. The performative, twisting flow of Horace's sociable long poems, his letters and satires that I read in translations (not by Pound) were much more my speed.

But I was hypnotized by *ABC of Reading* as a practical guide, with the commanding specificity of the "Exhibits" Pound assembled as examples. I could not resist the astounding confidence of his "Sequence of writers through whom the metamorphosis of English verse writing may be traced."

That "sequence of writers"—a list that goes from Chaucer and Villon to Rimbaud and Laforgue, with Shakespeare,

Landor, and Whitman in between—begins and ends with for-
eign languages. The seriousness and audacity of that nutty, pe-
dantic and (above all) craft-centered list in *The ABC of Reading*
affected my efforts in poetry deeply, as no university course, and
no reading of contemporary poetry, ever could.

As one answer to "Where did these books come from," I can
plead ignorance—specifically, my relative ignorance of con-
temporary poets and ideas that many poets in my generation
were studying in Creative Writing courses and MFA programs.
At Rutgers in my undergraduate literary set, our would-be-
bohemian pose was to be above such courses. That pretentious
resistance limited how much I knew about the poetry of my
time. In keeping with Pound's "sequence of writers" from Chau-
cer to Whitman and Laforgue I took not creative writing but
literature courses, where I read Dickinson, Yeats, Moore, and
Eliot but not Lowell or Bishop or Hayden. When I wandered
into books by living writers such as Thom Gunn, Allen Gins-
berg, or Alan Dugan, it was by chance, or guided by my friends
rather than teachers.

Meanwhile, gifted poets my age were students of poets
such as Denise Levertov or Robert Lowell. Many admired
poets taught writing in the preeminent MFA program at the
University of Iowa. At Stanford, where I landed, there was a
PhD program, not an MFA. What I learned from Yvor Win-
ters in Palo Alto was sixteenth-century poetry, the syntactical
melodies of John Dowland, Thomas Campion, George Gas-
coigne, and Fulke Greville. To his credit, Winters in his youth
had written the praises of Wallace Stevens and Marianne
Moore and other modernists when they were still unknown.
But he was also impossibly weird. He told his students in a

lyric poetry class that T. Sturge Moore was a better poet than William Butler Yeats. When other young poets were deep in the work of James Merrill or Adrienne Rich, I was memorizing poems by Ben Jonson and George Herbert, trying to draw my own lines from them to what I found in *Poetry*, *The Partisan Review*, and *The Paris Review*, thanks to the college library and to Stanford contemporaries like Robert Hass and James McMichael.

In *Sadness And Happiness* and *An Explanation of America*, I was not in rebellion against the poetry of my time so much as I was just not deeply into it.

But I shouldn't exaggerate. I did study intensely the idiom and iambic pentameters of Allen Ginsberg. Sometimes his blank verse was methodically regular, for example:

My books piled up before me for my use.

("TRANSCRIPTION FOR ORGAN MUSIC")

Sometimes, in my purposeful reading, I emphasized the Shakespearean blank verse I heard in Ginsberg's lines, unburying the meter by misquoting just a little, or accidentally on purpose:

America, when will we end the human war?
Go fuck yourself, you with your atom bomb.

("AMERICA")

Those poems were in my early edition of *Howl and Other Poems*, Ginsberg's first book, with a brief introduction by William Carlos Williams, who was a friend of Ginsberg's father Louis Ginsberg. I had by memory Williams's poem "Fine Work with Pitch and Copper":

Now they are resting
in the fleckless light
separately in unison

like the sacks
of sifted stone stacked
regularly by twos

about the flat roof
ready after lunch
to be opened and strewn

The copper in eight
foot strips has been
beaten lengthwise

down the center at right
angles and lies ready
to edge the coping

One still chewing
picks up a copper strip
and runs his eye along it.

This poem entered my memory in the unsystematic, performative way that has been at the center of poetry for me. The poem's three unpunctuated sentences, in order, perform an action I'll try to describe.

The account of roofing work generates an elegant, bravura, homemade definition by example of poetry itself. That the three units are clearly sentences, absolutely, without any marks of punctuation, but by virtue of what Robert Frost calls "sentence sounds" in a letter, is part of the demonstrated mastery of craft by Williams.

The first sentence elevates visual description into a musical prelude, beginning with the short "e" vowel of "resting" "fleckless" and "separately." From that initial key of "eh," the spoken, idiomatic flow of the grammar modulates into the "oo" sound of "unison," "twos," "roof," and "strewn." By pleasurable force of repetition, syntax transforms meaning, like a melody.

The middle, second sentence, with its passive voice ("has been / beaten lengthwise") could appear in an instruction manual for roofers—taking the poem's musical and descriptive flamboyance to another level of mastery, by disguising those qualities in an informative flatness. If understatement can be brought to an extreme, here it is—capped by a sly bit of end-rhyme on "coping / chewing" that introduces the final sentence, where mere visual description rises into the acutely observed, momentary, personal and social reality of "One still chewing"—one who gives himself the casual pleasure of smoothing the boundary, for a few seconds, between lunch and work. By noting that familiar nuance of behavior, the poet has revealed something human about the scene, running his practiced eye along it, expressed in a concluding musical flourish.

"Fine Work with Pitch and Copper" and Ginsberg's "America" share an expressive quality, somewhere between artful and unbound, or between being natural and showing off, that inspired my early efforts in poetry. I will add one more example, Robert Frost's "Provide, Provide," with its earworm closing stanza:

Better to go down dignified
With boughten friendship at your side
Than none at all. Provide, provide!

I didn't know enough about contemporary poetry to know that Ginsberg's lines and Williams's and Frost's were very different from one another, according to the experts. To my ear, those poets had a lot in common. All I knew enough to hear was their shared roots. (Williams says in *I Wanted to Write a Poem* that he had memorized the old-fashioned anthology *Palgrave's Treasury*.) Frost and Williams seemed similar to me, as a matter of idiom and line, in a way related to why I love the pentameters of Wallace Stevens and Elizabeth Bishop, as well as their free verse, but I lack much of an ear for the different formalism of W. H. Auden or James Merrill, based on a different kind of idiom.

I liked how Frost places the adjective "dignified" so it sounds kind of slangy or incorrect, jangling in a funny, appealing way with the rustic-sounding "boughten"—for me, playing spoken language into or against form, not different from how Ginsberg's pentameter line about the atom bomb uses "Go fuck yourself." "Boughten" and "fuck" don't only speak in the idiom of actual American speech, they speak *for* that idiom, with a social meaning.

I wrote most of *Sadness And Happiness* in London, as a young professor on early leave from Wellesley College. I based the poem partly on the way I talk, the ordinary speaking style or styles I had assimilated from my parents and their friends and my own friends, in Long Branch, New Jersey. There in England, writing not for publication but to amuse myself, distant from Wellesley but somehow not from Long Branch, it was fun to scramble together the personal, New Jersey voices, joke-telling voices of my parents and their friends, pizza parlor or classroom or basketball voices of my own friends, blending and jangling with the in-print voices of John Donne and Mad Magazine and

Vladimir Nabokov and Bill Griffith and Allen Ginsberg and
Emily Dickinson and Walt Kelly and William Blake:

V

or the things I see, driving
with you: houses and cars, trees,
grasses and birds; people, incidents
of the senses—like women and men, dusk

on a golf course, waving clubs
dreamily in slow practice-gestures
profiled against a sky layered
purpleish turquoise and gray, having

sport in the evening; or white
selvage of a mockingbird's gray
blur as he dabbles wings and tail
in a gutter—all in a way fraught,

full of emotion, and yet empty—
how can I say it?—all empty
of sadness and happiness, deep
blank passions, waiting like houses

and cars of a strange place,
a profound emptiness that came once
in the car, your cheekbone, lashes,
hair at my vision's edge, driving

VI

back from Vermont and then
into the iron dusk of Cambridge,

Central Square suddenly become
the most strange of places

as a Salvation Army band marches
down the middle, shouldering aside
the farting, evil-tempered traffic,
brass pitting its triplets and sixteenths

into the sundown fray of cops, gesturing
derelicts, young girls begging quarters,
shoppers and released secretaries, scruffy
workers and students, dropouts, children

whistling, gathering as the band
steps in place tootling and rumbling
in the square now, under an apocalypse
of green-and-pink sky, with paper

and filth spinning in the wind, crazy,
everyone—band, audience, city, lady
trumpeter fiddling spit-valve, John
Philip Sousa, me, Christianity, crazy

VII

and all empty except for you,
who look sometimes like a stranger;
as a favorite room, lake, picture
might look seen after years away,

your face at a new angle grows
unfamiliar and blank, love's face

perhaps, where I chose once to dream
again, but better, those past failures

"Some lovely, glorious Nothing," Susan,
Patricia, Celia, forgive me—God,
a girl in my street was called Half-
A-Buck, not right in her head . . .

The second-person "with you" at the beginning of this passage imitates Nabokov in *Speak, Memory*, which I was reading that year in London. The "glorious nothing" sounds to me a bit like Allen Ginsberg but it comes from John Donne. The farting apocalypse in Central Square certainly harks to Ginsberg. The "sundown fray" of the street and "having sport" of the golfers felt free to me, including old and new or high and low like the catalogue including "spit-valve" and "Christianity." For good or bad, probably some of each, the distance from home made it easier to yack, throwing things together by talking about them, as if aloud, or actually aloud.

The title "Sadness And Happiness," with its uppercase "A," was the name of a game Ellen Pinsky invented as a bedtime ritual for our small children. After a bedtime story, each child could choose which to tell first: one sad thing that happened that day or one happy thing. The game, which the kids loved, felt somehow related to the writing I was doing in the bracketed year away from home. That feeling, too, went into the omnivorous title poem.

Then we returned to Wellesley, and as a college professor in my thirties I had my first experience of a creative writing workshop: Barry Spacks, the poet teaching at MIT and my Wellesley neighbor, organized a group of poets. Barry and I were joined by Joyce Pesseroff, fresh from the MFA program at UC Irvine; my Wellesley colleague David Ferry; a new Wellesley part-time teacher Frank Bidart, a student of Robert Lowell's at Harvard. We began meeting once a week. Those sessions helped all of us, I think, in our different ways.

A month or two into the arrangement, there was an evening session when there was little or no work anyone wanted to present, so I made copies of "Sadness And Happiness," almost as a joke. My fellow poets took that draft of the poem seriously, suggesting places for revision. They understood, in interesting ways, what the grammar meant by pressing its way ahead through the formal divisions. That evening, poets who knew what they were talking about, including the authors of memorable books, gave me confidence in what I had been trying out, tentatively and in isolation, for the preceding year. By accepting what they read, my fellow-poets inspired my drastic or unruly first book.

And my second book, too. *An Explanation of America* tries to reach into some of the meaningful or unmeaning particulars of my particular American life, rationalized or jazzed, with segues and seams crisscrossing what I read or heard. Walt Whitman and Henny Youngman, Sonny Rollins and Willa Cather, Catullus and Lee Andrews, convening to sprawl under three commonplaces about the USA: Its Many Fragments, Its Great Emptiness, and Its Everlasting Possibility, each of the three with four named chapters, to make the most fluently divisible of numbers, twelve, like the clock or the calendar.

I can't claim that I wrote a prophetic book about my country, though I understand why the possibility has been suggested.

The realities of immigration and nativism, racism and Jew-hating, democracy and autocracy, cults and anti-intellectualism, all were visible, distinct, everyday presences. Elements of my personal history or character made me include them in my poem. A matter of circumstance and observation, not vision or prophesy.

Maybe *An Explanation of America* extended a kind of writing as far as I could bring it. Maybe certain unruly ways of writing—for example not "going in fear of abstractions," as Pound instructed—had served their purpose. I'm not sure how to describe the change, but my work took different directions. Different directions, but the same person with the same lifetime and ongoing needs. And nothing abandoned: these books are parts of my story. I am glad to have them together here, and I would be glad to read aloud anything in them, to anyone who might want to listen.

THE FIRST TWO BOOKS OF POEMS

SADNESS AND HAPPINESS

(1975)

I

The Time Of Year, The Time Of Day

Poem About People

The jaunty crop-haired graying
Women in grocery stores,
Their clothes boyish and neat,
New mittens or clean sneakers,

Clean hands, hips not bad still,
Buying ice cream, steaks, soda,
Fresh melons and soap—or the big
Balding young men in work shoes

And green work pants, beer belly
And white T-shirt, the porky walk
Back to the truck, polite; possible
To feel briefly like Jesus,

A gust of diffuse tenderness
Crossing the dark spaces
To where the dry self burrows
Or nests, something that stirs,

Watching the kinds of people
On the street for a while—
But how love falters and flags
When anyone's difficult eyes come

Into focus, terrible gaze of a unique
Soul, its need unlovable: my friend
In his divorced schoolteacher
Apartment, his own unsuspected

Paintings hung everywhere,
Which his wife kept in a closet—
Not, he says, that she wasn't
Perfectly right; or me, mis-hearing

My rock radio sing my self-pity:
"The Angels Wished Him Dead"—all
The hideous, sudden stare of self,
Soul showing through like the lizard

Ancestry showing in the frontal gaze
Of a robin busy on the lawn.
In the movies, when the sensitive
Young Jewish soldier nearly drowns

Trying to rescue the thrashing
Anti-semitic bully, swimming across
The river raked by nazi fire,
The awful part is the part truth:

Hate my whole kind, but me,
Love me for myself. The weather
Changes in the black of night,
And the dream-wind, bowling across

The sopping open spaces
Of roads, golf-courses, parking lots,
Flails a commotion
In the dripping treetops,

Tries a half-rotten shingle
Or a down-hung branch, and we
All dream it, the dark wind crossing
The wide spaces between us.

The Time Of Year,
The Time Of Day

One way I need you, the way I come to need
Our custom of speech, or need this other custom
Of speech in lines, is to alleviate
The weather, the time of year, the time of day.

I mean for instance the way the dusk in late
Winter or early spring recalls adolescence:
The pity of my comical unease
And vague depression on the long walk home

From the grim school through washed-out extra
   daylight
And the yellow light that waited in kitchen windows,
Daydreaming victories on the long parades
Of artificial brick and bare hydrangea.

But how cold in retrospect the afternoon
And evening even in July could seem,
Cold heralding that now those very hours

Are on the way, the very hours which one

Had better use, which may be what it is
About the time of year and the time of day,
Their burden of a promise but a promise
Limited, that sends folk huddling to their bodies

Or kitchens as colonizers of the day
And of the year, rough settlers who throughout
The stunning winter couple in a fury
To fill the brown width of their tillable plains.

Ceremony For Any Beginning

Against weather, and the random
Harpies—mood, circumstance, the laws
Of biography, chance, physics—
The unseasonable soul holds forth,
Eager for form as a renowned
Pedant, the emperor's man of worth,
Hereditary arbiter of manners.

Soul, one's life is one's enemy.
As the small children learn, what happens
Takes over, and what you were goes away.
They learn it in sardonic soft
Comments of the weather, when it sharpens
The hard surfaces of daylight: light
Winds, vague in direction, like blades

Lavishing their brilliant strokes
All over a wrecked house,
The nude wallpaper and the brute
Intelligence of the torn pipes.

Therefore when you marry or build
Pray to be untrue to the plain
Dominance of your own weather, how it keeps

Going even in the woods when not
A soul is there, and how it implies
Always that separate, cold
Splendidness, uncouth and unkind—
On chilly, unclouded mornings,
Torrential sunlight and moist air,
Leafage and solid bark breathing the mist.

Waiting

When the trains go by
The frozen ground shivers
Inwardly like an anvil.

The sky reaches down
Stiffly into the spaces
Among houses and trees.

A wisp of harsh air snakes
Upward between glove
And cuff, quickening

The sense of the life
Elsewhere of things, the things
You touched, maybe, numb

Handle of a rake; stone
Of a peach; soiled
Band-Aid; book, pants

Or shirt that you touched
Once in a store . . . less
The significant fond junk

Of someone's garage, and less
The cinder out of your eye—
Still extant and floating

In Sweden or a bird's crop—
Than the things that you noticed
Or not, watching from a train:

The cold wide river of things,
Going by like the cold
Children who stood by the tracks

Holding for no reason sticks
Or other things, waiting
For no reason for the trains.

December Blues

At the bad time, nothing betrays outwardly the harsh
    findings,
The studies and hospital records. Carols play.

Sitting upright in the transit system, the widowlike women
Wait, hands folded in their laps, as monumental as bread.

In the shopping center lots, lights mounted on cold
    standards
Tower and stir, condensing the blue vapour

Of the stars; between the rows of cars people in coats walk
Bundling packages in their arms or holding the hands of
    children.

Across the highway, where a town thickens by the tracks
With stores open late and creches in front of the churches,

Even in the bars a businesslike set of the face keeps off
The nostalgic pitfall of the carols, tugging. In bed,

How low and still the people lie, some awake, holding the
    carols
Consciously at bay, Oh Little Town, enveloped in unease.

Discretions Of Alcibiades

First frost is weeks off, but the prudent man
With house-plants on his front porch marks the season
And moves the potted *ficus* back indoors

While windows can be open for a while.
(The plant prefers a gradual transition.)
—The kid who did his homework, washed his face

And never wore tight pants, kept cherry bombs
And nasty photos in his briefcase (think:
A seventh-grader with a briefcase)—Hantman,

In Student Council with his red-hot bag:
His picture of a lady on all fours,
A Great Dane on her back, was not for sale.

And though he may have sold a bomb or two,
And must have set some off, I like to think
He preferred, like Presidents, their deep reserve.

Speaking of gradual transitions, "plant
Prefers" of course is only an expression.
You might say that the plant prefers to die,

Or wishes it were home, in Borneo,
Preferring never to have seen a window.
The stars are similar: "The wheeling Bear,

One white eye on the Pleiads, rolls another
At glowering Orion." Autumn stars.
On this first chilly dusk, a furry bat,

Warm-blooded, dips and flutters in the sky.
(Some constellations might be called, "The Bat.")
The roles are arbitrary too. The man

Who sleeps with Socrates and Leontes' wife,
Who knocks the cocks from his own effigies,
Or not, simply prefers—to use another

Expression—to hide his briefcase in a bomb.
Consider gods and heroes, how they merge:
(I speak as one believing in the gods,

Especially in quick, reflective Hermes,
So sensitive and practical—like a thief,
Or like long-suffering, shrewd Odysseus).

Apollo, sullen and glamorous obverse
Of Hermes, shrouds himself in dark, or shines,
Like bold Achilles in his tent—or out,

As he prefers. All one. Tithonus, too,
And Alcibiades, balling Lady Luck
Until she dried him up. When people say

"How was your summer?" who is there alive
Who wouldn't like to change sides, go to Sparta
Like Alcibiades, cut your hair, live clean . . .

And then knock up the king's wife on the sly.
That's where the inner briefcase is revealed:
He hoped his heir would be the King of Sparta—

More screwing with Fortuna, man with goddess . . .
From a god's point of view, it is perhaps
Disgusting, if exciting in a way,

Like a dog doing a lady from behind.
The sundry dogs from along the road prefer
To conduct ferocious gang-fucks in a field:

Dogs Only, in the end-of-summer fest.
But people, on Cape Cod, the Costa Brava,
Borneo, emulate gods and goddesses:

Rubbing their skin with oil, they sun it brown
Until they all are Spaniard, Jew or Greek—
Wear sandals; ply their boat; keep simple house

Cooking red meat or fish on open fires;
Market for salt; and dance to tinkly music.

Tennis

TO HOWARD WILCOX

I. The Service
The nerve to make a high toss and the sense
Of when the ball is there; and then the nerve
To cock your arm back all the way, not rigid

But loose and ready all the way behind
So that the racket nearly or really touches
Your back far down; and all the time to see

The ball, the seams and letters on the ball
As it seems briefly at its highest point
To stop and hover—keeping these in mind,

The swing itself is easy; forgetting cancer,
Or panic learning how to swim or walk,
Forgetting what the score is, names of plants,

And your first piece of ass, you throw the racket
Easily through Brazil, coins, mathematics
And *haute cuisine* to press the ball from over

And a slight slice at two o'clock or less,
Enough to make it loop in accurately
As, like a fish in water flicking itself

Away, your mind takes up the next concern
With the arm, ball, racket still pressing down
And forward and across your obedient body.

II. Forehand

Straightforwardness can be a cruel test,
A kind of stagefright threatening on the cold
And level dais, a time of no excuses.

But think about the word *"stroke,"* how it means
What one does to a cat's back, what a brush
Does through a woman's long hair. Think about

The racket pressing, wiping, guiding the ball
As you stay on it, dragging say seven strings
Across the ball, the top edge leading off

To give it topspin. Think about the ball
As a loaf of bread, you hitting every slice.
Pull back the racket well behind you, drop it

And lift it, meeting the ball well out in front
At a point even with your left hip, stroking
To follow through cross-court. The tarnished coin

Of "follow through," the cat, the loaf of bread,
"Keep your eye on the ball," the dull alloy
Of homily, simile and coach's lore

As maddening, and as helpful, as the Fool
Or Æsop's *Fables*, the coinage of advice:
This is the metal that is never spent.

III. Backhand

Here, panic may be a problem; and in the clench
From back to jaw in panic you may come
Too close and struggling strike out with your arm,

Trying to make the arm do everything,
And failing as the legs and trunk resist.
All of your coinages, and your nerve, may fail . . .

What you need is the Uroborus, the serpent
Of energy and equilibrium,
Its tail between its jaws, the female circle

Which makes it easy: all is all, the left
Reflects the right, and if you change the grip
To keep your hand and wrist behind the racket

You suddenly find the swing is just the same
As forehand, except you hit it more in front
Because your arm now hangs in front of you

And not behind. You simply change the grip
And with a circular motion from the shoulder,
Hips, ankles, and knees, you sweep the inverted swing.

IV. Strategy

Hit to the weakness. All things being equal
Hit crosscourt rather than down the line, because
If you hit crosscourt back to him, then he

Can only hit back either towards you (crosscourt)
Or parallel to you (down the line), but never
Away from you, the way that you can hit

Away from him if he hits down the line.
Besides, the net is lowest in the middle,
The court itself is longest corner-to-corner,

So that a crosscourt stroke is the most secure,
And that should be your plan, the plan you need
For winning—though only when hitting from the
    baseline:

From closer up, hit straight ahead, to follow
The ball to net; and from the net hit shrewdly,
To get him into trouble so he will hit

An error, or a cripple you can kill.
If he gets you in trouble, hit a lob,
And make it towering to make it hard

For him to smash from overhead and easy
For you to have the time to range the backcourt,
Bouncing in rhythm like a dog or seal

Ready to catch an object in mid-air
And rocking its head—as with your plan in mind
You arrange yourself to lob it back, and win.

V. Winning

Call questionable balls his way, not yours;
You lose the point but have your concentration,
The grail of self-respect. Wear white. Mind losing.

Walk, never run, between points: it will save
Your breath, and hypnotize him, and he may think
That you are tired, until your terrible

Swift sword amazes him. By understanding
Your body, you will conquer your fatigue.
By understanding your desire to win

And all your other desires, you will conquer
Discouragement. And you will conquer distraction
By understanding the world, and all its parts.

II

Sadness And Happiness

Sadness And Happiness

I

That they have no earthly measure
is well known—the surprise is
how often it becomes impossible
to tell one from the other in memory:

the sadness of past failures, the strangely
happy—doubtless corrupt—
fondling of them. Crude, empty
though the terms are, they do

organize life: sad American
house-hunting couples with kids
and small savings visit Model Homes
each Sunday for years; humble,

they need closet space, closet
space to organize life . . . in older
countries people seem to be happy
with less closet space. Empty space,

I suppose, also explains *post
coitum triste,* a phenomenon
which on reflection I am happy
to find rare in my memory—not,

II

God knows, that sex isn't crucial,
a desire to get more or better
must underlie the "pain" and "bliss"
of sonnets—or is it a need to *do* better:

A girl touched my sleeve, once,
held it, deep-eyed; life too at times
has come up, looked into my face,
My Lord, how like you this? And I?

Always distracted by some secret
movie camera or absurd audience
eager for cliches, *Ivanhoe,* de blues,
Young Man With A Horn, the star

tripping over his lance, quill, phallic
symbol or saxophone—miserable,
these absurd memories of failure
to see anything but oneself,

my pride, my consciousness, my shame, my
sickly haze of Romance—sick too
the root of joy? "Bale" and "bliss" merge
in a Petrarchist grin, that sleeve's burden

III

or chivalric trophy to bear as
emblem or mark of the holy
idiot: know ye, this natural stood
posing amiss while the best prizes

of life bounced off his vague
pate or streamed between his legs—
did Korsh, Old Russia's bedlam-sage,
enjoy having princesses visit his cell?

Would they dote on me as I shake out
a match, my fountain pen in the same
hand, freckling my dim brow with ink?
Into his muttered babble they read tips

on the market, court, marriage—I too
mutter: *Fool, fool*! or *Death*!
or *Joy*! Well, somewhere in the mind's mess
feelings are genuine, someone's

mad voice undistracted, clarity
maybe of motive and precise need
like an enamelled sky, cool
blue of Indian Summer, happiness

IV

like the sex-drowsy saxophones
rolling flatted thirds of the blues
over and over, rocking the dulcet
rhythms of regret, Black music

which tumbles loss over in the mouth
like a moist bone full of marrow;
the converse is a good mood grown
too rich, like dark water steeping

willow-roots in the shade, spotted
with sun and slight odor of dirt
or death, insane quibbles of self-
regard . . . better to mutter *fool*

or feel solaces of unmerited
Grace, like a road of inexplicable
dells, rises and lakes, found
in a flat place of no lakes—or feel

the senses: cheese, bread, tart
apples and wine, broiling acres
of sunflowers in Spain, mansards
in Vermont, painted shay and pard,

V

or the things I see, driving
with you: houses and cars, trees,
grasses and birds; people, incidents
of the senses—like women and men, dusk

on a golf course, waving clubs
dreamily in slow practice-gestures
profiled against a sky layered
purpleish turquoise and gray, having

sport in the evening; or white
selvage of a mockingbird's gray
blur as he dabbles wings and tail
in a gutter—all in a way fraught,

full of emotion, and yet empty—
how can I say it?—all empty
of sadness and happiness, deep
blank passions, waiting like houses

and cars of a strange place,
a profound emptiness that came once
in the car, your cheekbone, lashes,
hair at my vision's edge, driving

VI

back from Vermont and then
into the iron dusk of Cambridge,
Central Square suddenly become
the most strange of places

as a Salvation Army band marches
down the middle, shouldering aside
the farting, evil-tempered traffic,
brass pitting its triplets and sixteenths

into the sundown fray of cops, gesturing
derelicts, young girls begging quarters,
shoppers and released secretaries, scruffy
workers and students, dropouts, children

whistling, gathering as the band
steps in place tootling and rumbling
in the square now, under an apocalypse
of green-and-pink sky, with paper

and filth spinning in the wind, crazy,
everyone—band, audience, city, lady
trumpeter fiddling spit-valve, John
Philip Sousa, me, Christianity, crazy

VII

and all empty except for you,
who look sometimes like a stranger;
as a favorite room, lake, picture
might look seen after years away,

your face at a new angle grows
unfamiliar and blank, love's face
perhaps, where I chose once to dream
again, but better, those past failures—

"Some lovely, glorious Nothing," Susan,
Patricia, Celia, forgive me—God,
a girl in my street was called Half-
A-Buck, not right in her head . . .

how happy I would be, or else
decently sad, with no past: you
only and no foolish ghosts
urging me to become some redeeming

Jewish-American Shakespeare
(or God knows what they expect,
Longfellow) and so excuse my thorny
egotism, my hard-ons of self-concern,

VIII

melodramas and speeches
of myself, crazy in love with
my status as a sad young man: dreams
of myself old, a vomit-stained

ex-Jazz-Immortal, collapsed
in a phlegmy Bowery doorway
on Old Mr. Boston lemon-flavored
gin or on cheap wine—that romantic

fantasy of my future bumhood
excused all manner of lies, fumbles,
destructions, even this minute, "*Mea
culpa*!" I want to scream, stealing

the podium to address the band,
the kids, the old ladies awaiting
buses, the glazed winos (who accomplished
my dream while I got you, and art,

and daughters): "Oh you city of
undone deathcrotches! Terrible
the film of green brainpus! Fog
of corruption at the great shitfry! No

IX

grease-trickling sink
of disorder in your depressed
avenues is more terrible
than these, and not your whole

aggregate of pollution
is more heavy than the measure
of unplumbed muttering
remorse, shame, inchoate pride

and nostalgia in any one
sulphur-choked, grit-breathing
citizen of the place. . . ." Sad,
the way one in part enjoys

air pollution, relishes
millennial doom, headlines,
even the troubles of friends—
or, OK, enjoys hearing

and talking about them, anyway—
to be whole-hearted is rare;
changing as the heart does, is it
the heart, or the sun emerging from

X

or going behind a cloud,
or a change somewhere in my eyes?
Terrible, to think that mere pretty
scenery—or less, the heraldic shape

of an oak leaf drifting down
curbside waters in the sun, pink
bittersweet among the few last
gray sad leaves of the fall—can bring

joy, or fail to. Shouldn't I vow
to seek only within myself
my only hire? Or not? All my senses,
like beacon's flame, counsel gratitude

for the two bright-faced girls
crossing the Square, beauty a light
or intelligence, no quarters for them,
long legs flashing bravely above

the grime—it is as if men were to
go forth plumed in white
uniforms and swords; how could we
ever aspire to such smartness,

XI

such happy grace? Pretty enough
plumage and all, a man in the bullshit
eloquence of his sad praises stumbles,
fumbles: *fool*. It is true, wonder

does indeed hinder love and hate,
and one can behold well with eyes
only what lies beneath him—
so that it takes more than eyes

to see well anything that is worth
loving; that is the sad part, the senses
are not visionary, they can tug
downward, even in pure joy—

trivial joy, the deep solid crack
of the bat. A sandlot home run
has led me to clown circling
the diamond as though cheered

by a make-believe audience
of thousands (you, dead poets, friends,
old coaches and teachers, everyone
I ever knew) cheering louder as I tip

XII

my imaginary, ironic hat and blow
false kisses crossing home, happiness
impure and oddly memorable as the sad
agony of recalled errors lived over

before sleep, poor throws awry
or the ball streaming through,
between my poor foolish legs, crouching
amazéd like a sot. Sport—woodmanship,

ball games, court games—has its cruel
finitude of skill, good-and-bad, as does
the bizarre art of words: confirmation
of a good word, *polvo*, dust, reddish gray

powder of the ballfield, *el polvo*
rising in pale puffs to glaze lightly
the brown ankles and brown bare feet in
Cervantes' poem of the girl dancing, all

dust now, poet, girl. It is intolerable
to think of my daughters, too, dust—
el polvo—or you whose invented game,
Sadness and Happiness, soothes them

XIII

to sleep: can you tell me one sad
thing that happened today, Can you think
of one happy thing to tell me that
happened to you today, organizing

life—not you too dust like the poets,
dancers, athletes, their dear skills
and the alleged glittering gaiety of
Art which, in my crabwise scribbling hand,

no less than Earth the change of all
changes breedeth, art and life
both inconstant mothers, in whose
fixed cold bosoms we lie fixed,

desperate to devise anything, any
sadness or happiness, only
to escape the clasped coffinworm
truth of eternal art or marmoreal

infinite nature, twin stiff
destined measures both manifested
by my shoes, coated with dust or dew which no
earthly measure will survive.

III

Persons

To My Father

FOR MILFORD S. PINSKY

The glazed surface of the world, dusk
And three mallard that land
In the dim lake, each

Scudding in a bright oval . . .
What chance, man, for the thin
Halting qualities of the soul?

Call this, prologue to an explanation,
Something like the way Uncle Joe Winograd
With a carpenter's flat silence

Might act on some given stretch
Of Uncle Italo Tarantola's lifelong
Lawyerly expanding monologue.

What I wanted, was to dwell
Here in the brain as though
At my bench, as though in a place

Like the live ongoing shop—
Between kitchen and factory—
Of a worker in wood or in leather:

Implements ranged in sizes and shapes,
The stuff itself stacked up
In the localized purposeful clutter

Of work, the place itself smelling
Of the hide, sawdust or whatever.
I wanted the exact words;

I wanted the way to pronounce
Evenly the judgment which a man
Who is quiet holds back as distinct

But not final in the presence
Of a good talker. I a good talker
Ask you a quiet man to recall the inside

Of a shop, glassdust and lenses
Everywhere, broken eyeglasses, forms
And odd pieces of paper, voices

Like phones ringing, tools
Broken and whole everywhere, mail
Unread, the sign—"Milford S." or

"Robert"—hanging like a straight face . . .
Surface, tyranny of the world visible,
Images that spread outward

From the brain like lines crazing—
Or like brief silvery ovals
That glide over the dark,

Ethereal, yet each wingbeat
Firm in time, of more
Substance than this, this mothlike

Stirring of words, work or affection.

Old Woman

Not even in darkest August,
When the mysterious insects
Marry loudly in the black weeds
And the woodbine, limp after rain,
In the cooled night is more fragrant,
Do you gather in any slight
Harvest to yourself. Deep whispers
Of slight thunder, horizons off,
May break your thin sleep, but awake,
You cannot hear them. Harsh gleaner
Of children, grandchildren—remnants
Of nights now forever future—
Your dry, invisible shudder
Dies on this porch where, uninflamed,
You dread the oncoming seasons,
Repose in the electric night.

Library Scene

TO P.M.S.

Under the ceiling of metal stamped like plaster
And below the ceiling fan, in the brown lustre

Someone is reading, in the sleepy room
Alert, her damp cheek balanced on one palm,

With knuckles loosely holding back the pages
Or fingers waiting lightly at their edges.

Her eyes are like the eyes of someone attending
To a fragile work, familiar and demanding—

Some work of delicate surfaces or threads.
Someone is reading the way a rare child reads,

A kind of changeling reading for love of reading,
For love and for the course of something leading

Her child's intelligent soul through its inflection:
A force, a kind of loving work or action.

Someone is reading in a deepening room
Where something happens, something that will come

To happen again, happening as many times
As she is reading in as many rooms.

What happens outside that calm like water braiding
Over green stones? The ones of little reading

Or who never read for love, are many places.
They are in the house of power, and many houses

Reading as they do, doing what they do.
Or it happens that they come, at times, to you

Because you are somehow someone that they need:
They come to you and you tell them how you read.

First Early Mornings Together

Waking up over the candy store together
We hear birds waking up below the sill
And slowly recognize ourselves, the weather,
The time, and the birds that rustle there until

Down to the street as fog and quiet lift
The pigeons from the wrinkled awning flutter
To reconnoiter, mutter, stare and shift
Pecking by ones or twos the rainbowed gutter.

The Sentences

Reading the sentences, November sun
Touching the avenues, offices, the station,
I saw you pass me on a street, your face
Was pink with cold, cold windows flashed, the stores
And cars were like—mythology—, the street
Itself was glamorous and lost, it was
As though I never knew you yet somehow knew
That this was you, a sentence interdicted
The present, it said, *you never knew,* you passed,
Leaves coppery and quick as lizards moved
Around your delicate ankles; November sun
Lay on the sidewalk, ordinary and final
As the sentences too flat for any poem.

Daughter

I
She thinks about skeletons,
Admires their symmetry,
Responding with fear
To the implied movement
And the near-absence of expression.
In the museum
Of natural history
She pressed up close
To the smaller ones;
But shook, studying the tall
Scaffolding of dinosaurs
From the next room.
Back home, sitting in the john
With the door open
She claims to see, in a mirror
Down the dark hall, her own.

II

At certain times, midway
In a meal, or feeling
The dried mucus of her nose
She stares nowhere like a cat.
It is not quite the same
As the damp sensual trance
Of her thumb. It does not
Seem to be thought, nor
The deep stare of a cat
Concentrating on a noise
Or a smell. It is like a cat
Staring nowhere. When she comes
Out of it or is interrupted
A great emptiness flares,
Of profound privacy,
Like a good Christian's death.

III

With people, she deals oddly.
Normally too savage for bribes,
She attaches herself
In the way of a feudal tenant
To a grandma, overweight,
Spendthrift. The vassal
Declares prices,
Then haggles for a while.
She watches the two
Parents as they watch her

Pleasing herself with cheap
Toys and half-eaten sweets.
Chattering as two equals,
Nicole who calls herself "Mary"
And the woman nobody loves enough
Trot downtown for their perms.

IV

Like most children
She paints openly and well,
Somewhat like Henri Rousseau.
She and her friends paint
With a mild firmness
Of attention. Their great
Interest when they discuss
Paintings they have made
Seems partly affected:
A habit, maybe, grown
From the ineluctable
Deal that their kind make.
Is the painting also
Part of the deal? Often, she
Smears over her work, thick
Strokes, as for painting a wall.

V

She chats quietly
With a few cronies

On the subject of death.
They all have something to say,
Her contribution being
To list her close family
In correct order of age,
Declaring that we will die
In the same order. Nobody
Disagrees. *I know it,*
They say, *I know it.* One
Tells about graves. And then
They drift off the subject
Like that many businesslike
Starlings, flying away
From one tree among trees.

The Personal Devil

Ink, fire, quintuple mirrors—
By means bizarre enough,
I convoked the multiple eye
And saw from claw to scruff
The growth that Being nurtured:
The subtle bully whose Days—
His furies and lackeys and bearers—
Hang like the dozing flies
Whose billions in bog or orchard
Gorge with a daylong sigh.

The devices I arrayed
Conjured features like mine,
A familiar shape that I
Denied—denied as the bane
Of myself, the multifarious
Event that pulls my face
To its own. As I watched it fade
I saw myself take place,
Crystalline, in the iris
Of the huge, dissolving eye.

Spelunker

With flecks of web like foam
Still clinging to his brow and back
The deep explorer in his dream
Of rescue turns to seek

The faces of his friends
Already, as his arms come out
Into their cheering hands
Pulling him to the light

(Which thanks to certain drugs
Will not offend his eyes or skin)
And they will all be there; his legs
Will still be dangling down

Into the simple depth
(No symbol, no Womb or Self or Grave,
Neither his birth nor death
But a confusing cave

Where he is hurt and lost),
His feet still hanging in the dark
When to his mouth which they have kissed
The friends will hold a drink

Miraculously bright and cool,
The elixir of his dream,
His dream which marks the pall
Of darkness with cool stars for him,

Hallucinations which he knows
Are common in his plight
And which he now construes
As will-to-live, a faith in light

Surviving, so that he has come
To welcome this false Zodiac
Because it is his dream
Of rescue: for the sake

Of untrue lights to climb
Or burrow the expanding darkness
Which also is his dream
Of rescue, or the dream's dark likeness.

The Generation Before

TO FRANK BIDART

The wind blew. Some days, rain
Falling the size of nickels
Splashed up over the curb.
There were hats for that, and for sun
Too, frying shoeleather in its hot cycles.
Flesh was a poor garb,

So poor, the people were quaint—
Muffled up into their high cars
Or their quaint bulky clothing.
In the prolonged slap-happy Lent
Of the times, harder than yours,
Eating or asleep, breathing,

They got by in their manner, at times
Made Carnival in hotel bars,
At ball games or the track. In photographs,
In films, even in their haberdashery, games
And swank gear (cases, lighters,
Syphons, clips, objects for looks or laughs

Of glass, pigskin, malachite)
They survive as a vague murmur of style,
The nostalgic false life of a face
Shining from a snapshot. Time will not
Light gently on those fathers. They will fall
Sick in the lungs and the heart, hapless

In a motel, swearing at their own lost
Flickery past, craving a field
Empty and large, the growth pale and recent
Over the plow-twisting tangle of the past—
The grasses coarse, unculled,
The impossible field of the present.

IV

The Street Of
Furthest Memory

The Street Of
Furthest Memory

The street flails
old substances, a chaff
of felt, beaver-board,

slate shingles, tarpaper—plain
or made to resemble masonry
and brick—, oilcloth, sharkskin.

In a film of rain, the street
shines. Luncheonette,
lot, shoemaker,

They get clearer
in the rain, a spring rain
patched with sun,

the bright drops on glass,
on awnings of canvas, on cars
moving down the street

as the awnings flap,
flickering like a torn
film, coupe and sedan passing

to beyond your earliest
memory, on the street
out of memory, the sweet

street flailing its
lost substances, tangling
off as though thrown

from the spinning black
reel, unthreading rapidly, like
panic flailing the street.

Long Branch, New Jersey

Everything is regional,
And this is where I was born, dear,
And conceived,
And first moved to tears,
And last irritated to the same point.

It is bounded on three sides by similar places
And on one side by vast, uncouth houses
A glum boardwalk and,
As we say, The Beach.

I stand here now
At the corner of Third Avenue and Broadway
Waiting for you to come by in a car,
And count the red carlights
That rush through a fine rain
To where Broadway's two branches—North
Broadway and South Broadway—both reach
To the trite, salt, welcoming ocean.

Doctor Frolic

Felicity the healer isn't young
And you don't look him up unless you need him.
Clown's eyes, Pope's nose, a mouth for dirty stories,
He made his bundle in the Great Depression

And now, a jovial immigrant success
In baggy pinstripes, he winks and wheezes gossip,
Village stories that could lift your hair
Or lance a boil; the small town dirt, the dope,

The fishy deals and incestuous combinations,
The husband and the wife of his wife's brother,
The hospital contract, the certificate . . .
A realist and hardy omnivore,

He strolls the jetties when the month is right
With a knife and lemons in his pocket, after
Live mussels from among the smelly rocks,
Preventative of impotence and goitre.

And as though the sight of tissue healing crooked
Pleased him, like the ocean's vaginal taste,
He'll stitch your thumb up so it shows for life.
And where he once was the only quack in town

We all have heard his half-lame joke, the one
About the operation that succeeded,
The tangy line that keeps that clever eye
So merry in the punchinello face.

Pleasure Pier

With noises meaningful and vague as ever
The surf goes through its motions of attack.
Black water foams and comes erect and charges
White up the dark beach and collapses back to black.

Black under my feet, it sucks the kelp-haired pilings
That hold Convention Hall's Venetian folly
Up over the waters. The November air,
The boardwalk's void perspective, the melancholy

Of minarets and blistered stucco are blatant,
Crude as my crude vague needs, old hopes that dwell
On a violent urgency of color—blue mane
Of a horse frozen on the carousel,

A shooting-gallery bear whose eyes glare purple.
Among the sleeping pinballs and arcades
My boyhood lurks, as the phantom from a film
That the locale helps me dream. Hot-eyed, he wades

The boatride's oily channel, sleeps curled up
Among gears and pipes like viscera. In his arms
As he hurries through the tunnels of the Fun House
Is the Girl, the virgin whom he never harms.

Saved, she can't look when in the final scene
He dies in flames that throw their stagey lights
Out onto the water, the weary muttering waves
That pulled and worried at his prison's roots.

The Destruction Of
Long Branch

When they came out with artificial turf
I went back home with a thousand miles.

I dug a trench by moonlight from the ocean
And let it wash in quietly

And make a brackish quicksand which the tide
Sluiced upward from the streets and ditches.

The downtown that the shopping centers killed,
The garden apartments, the garages,

The station, the Little Africa on (so help me)
Liberty Street, the nicer sections,

All settled gently in a drench of sand
And sunk with a minimum of noise.

The hollow of the shut-down movie house
Made bubbles. Wooden porches crumbled

But ranch homes in the new developments,
Tilting a little, slipped in whole.

I pushed back pieces that floated up: one gash
Of neon, the martini glass

That winked outside a mafia hotel;
A gas pump; a bouquet of socks

From Woolley's window (I even kept a few);
The pinball from my grandpa's bar.

I laid out hills and ridges, and with a brush
I creosoted lumps of sewage

Where the school had shat its plumbing as it went.
I fitted my carpet on the crust

(That made-in-Japan grass went on like magic)
With a neat margin at the beach,

And I still had half the night. "How great," I said . . .
Then, since forgiving had been fun

I thought I'd leave a monument or two.
Cautiously elegiac, I dug

Some scenes back up to compose my parkland vistas:
Benches and gloomy vegetation,

Some things already dead, an abandoned boardwalk,
Some weather, an unfilled foundation—

With a brush of huckleberry or a ragged fern,
Cabbagey growth along a curb,

Thin flags of sumac from a vacant lot
Avid in a tearing rain.

The Beach Women

In the fierce peak of the day it's quietly they wade
With spread arms into the blue breakers rushing white
And swim seemingly with no tension, the arms
Curved, the head's gestures circular and slow.

They walk dripping back into the air
Of nineteen-fifty-five smiling downward from the glare
As if modestly, as they move daintily over the sand
Shaking their hair, tingling, taking it easy.

The beach flushes and broils, shapes ripple
In the waves of heat over it and the cold sea-water
Dries on their arms and legs and their suits, too,
Drying out stretched over their bottoms

In the luxury of sun flowering everywhere. The delicate
Salt glazing their skin they dissolve in oil.
Holiday colors throb on suits, towels, blankets,
Footwear, loose robes, bottles, carriers of straw,

Bright magazines and books, gear feminine and abundant
The whole overwhelming with a sense less of sex than
    gender,
The great oval blanks of their sunglasses hypnotic,
Flashing anonymous glamour over their cards, books or
    gossip.

It was Irving Stone they read, John O'Hara or Herman
    Wouk
Or the decade's muse of adultery: Grace Metalious.
With her picture in *Time,* floppy dungarees, no bra,
Retrospectively a seer, a social critic—

No doubt the cabana-boys weren't always lying
About their own ladies, mistresses whose husbands
Came down from New York to tip big on the week-end—
Like Mrs. F, strawberry-blond Italian . . .

What did she carry down to the sand all summer
But Wouk's *Caine Mutiny,* the earnest young sailors
Behaving like so many Jews, coming over guilty
Because they hadn't let Hitler as Lloyd Nolan

Played by Joe McCarthy send them under the waves.
Good for Grace, writing about "lust" with her flat
Characters and her big breasts. What did Mrs. F
Sunning at the shore fifteen years ago, or anyone,

Think about Caryl Chessman, Chaplin, Lucky Luciano,
Ike and the Rosenbergs? What can I recall? Women,
Moving in the sparkle of the sidewalk, blinding
Even in the reverse colors of the afterimage

Outside the drugstore where I worked, no cabana
    Lancelot,
Grateful for a wet cuddle with a chubby majorette.
I made club sandwiches and sundaes, on dark days
    purveyed
Dozens of copies of *Confidential*: "Victor Mature

Locked Me In A Cage" and "Russ Tamblyn's All Girl Party"
Cheered them up while the rain slashed gray
Soaking the boardwalk and gleaming on cars.
On those days I admired their tans, white dresses,

And pink oval fingernails on brown hands, and sold them
Perfume and lipstick, aspirins, throat lozenges and Tums,
Tampax, newspapers and paperback books—brave stays
Against boredom, discomfort, death and old age.

V

Essay On Psychiatrists

Essay On Psychiatrists

I. Invocation
It's crazy to think one could describe them—
Calling on reason, fantasy, memory, eyes and ears—
As though they were all alike any more

Than sweeps, opticians, poets or masseurs.
Moreover, they are for more than one reason
Difficult to speak of seriously and freely,

And I have never (even this is difficult to say
Plainly, without foolishness or irony)
Consulted one for professional help, though it happens

Many or most of my friends have—and that,
Perhaps, is why it seems urgent to try to speak
Sensibly about them, about the psychiatrists.

II. Some Terms

"Shrink" is a misnomer. The religious
Analogy is all wrong, too, and the old,
Half-forgotten jokes about Viennese accents

And beards hardly apply to the good-looking woman
In boots and a knit dress, or the man
Seen buying the Sunday *Times* in mutton-chop

Whiskers and expensive jogging shoes.
In a way I suspect that even the terms "doctor"
And "therapist" are misnomers; the patient

Is not necessarily "sick." And one assumes
That no small part of the psychiatrist's
Role is just that: to point out misnomers.

III. Proposition

These are the first citizens of contingency.
Far from the doctrinaire past of the old ones,
They think in their prudent meditations

Not about ecstasy (the soul leaving the body)
Nor enthusiasm (the god entering one's person)
Nor even about sanity (which means

Health, an impossible perfection)
But ponder instead relative truth and the warm
Dusk of amelioration. The cautious

Young augurs with their family-life, good books
And records and foreign cars believe
In amelioration—in that, and in suffering.

IV. A Lakeside Identification

Yes, crazy to suppose one could describe them—
And yet, there was this incident: at the local beach
Clouds of professors and the husbands of professors

Swam, dabbled or stood to talk with arms folded
Gazing at the lake . . . and one of the few townsfolk there,
With no faculty status—a matter-of-fact, competent,

Catholic woman of twenty-seven with five children
And a first-rate body—pointed her finger
At the back of one certain man and asked me,

"Is that guy a psychiatrist?" and by god he was! "Yes,"
She said, "He *looks* like a psychiatrist."
Grown quiet, I looked at his pink back, and thought.

V. Physical Comparison With Professors And Others

Pink and a bit soft-bodied, with a somewhat jazzy
Middle-class bathing suit and sandy sideburns, to me
He looked from the back like one more professor.

And from the front, too—the boyish, unformed carriage
Which foreigners always note in American men, combined
As in a professor with that liberal, quizzical,

Articulate gaze so unlike the more focused, more
Tolerant expression worn by a man of action (surgeon,
Salesman, athlete). On closer inspection was there,

Perhaps, a self-satisfied or benign air, a studied
Gentleness toward the child whose hand he held loosely?
Absurd to speculate; but then—the woman saw *something*.

VI. Their Seriousness, With Further Comparisons

In a certain sense, they are not serious.
That is, they are serious—useful, deeply helpful,
Concerned—only in the way that the pilots of huge

Planes, radiologists, and master mechanics can,
At their best, be serious. But however profound
The psychiatrists may be, they are not serious the way

A painter may be serious beyond pictures, or a
    businessman
May be serious beyond property and cash—or even
The way scholars and surgeons are serious, each rapt

In his work's final cause, contingent upon nothing:
Beyond work; persons; recoveries. And this is fitting:
Who would want to fly with a pilot who was *serious*

About getting to the destination safely? Terrifying idea—
That a pilot could over-extend, perhaps try to fly
Too well, or suffer from Pilot's Block; of course,

It may be that (just as they must not drink liquor
Before a flight) they undergo regular, required check-ups
With a psychiatrist, to prevent such things from
    happening.

VII. Historical (*The Bacchae*)

Madness itself, as an idea, leaves us confused—
Incredulous that it exists, or cruelly facetious,
Or stricken with a superstitious awe as if bound

By the lost cults of Trebizond and Pergamum . . .
The most profound study of madness is found
In the *Bacchae* of Euripides, so deeply disturbing

That in Cambridge, Massachusetts the players
Evaded some of the strongest unsettling material
By portraying poor sincere, fuddled, decent Pentheus

As a sort of fascistic bureaucrat—but it is Dionysus
Who holds rallies, instills exaltations of violence,
With his leopards and atavistic troops above law,

Reason and the good sense and reflective dignity
Of Pentheus—Pentheus, humiliated, addled, made to
    suffer
Atrocity as a minor jest of the smirking God.

When Bacchus's Chorus (who call him "most gentle"!)
    observe:
"Ten thousand men have ten thousand hopes; some fail,
Some come to fruit, but the happiest man is he

Who gathers the good of life day by day"—as though
Life itself were enough—does that mean, to leave
    ambition?
And is it a kind of therapy, or truth? Or both?

VIII. A Question

On the subject of madness the *Bacchae* seems,
On the whole, more *pro* than *contra*. The Chorus
Says of wine, "There is no other medicine for misery";

When the Queen in her ecstasy—or her enthusiasm?—
Tears her terrified son's arm from his body, or bears
His head on her spear, she remains happy so long

As she remains crazy; the God himself (who bound
   fawnskin
To the women's flesh, armed them with ivy arrows
And his orgies' livery) debases poor Pentheus first,

Then leads him to mince capering towards female Death
And dismemberment: flushed, grinning, the grave young
King of Thebes pulls at a slipping bra-strap, simpers

Down at his turned ankle. *Pentheus*: "Should I lift up
Mount Cithæron—Bacchae, mother and all?"
Dionysus: "Do what you want to do. Your mind

Was unstable once, but now you sound more sane,
You are on your way to great things." The question is,
Which is the psychiatrist: Pentheus, or Dionysus?

IX. Pentheus As Psychiatrist

With his reasonable questions Pentheus tries
To throw light on the old customs of savagery.
Like a brave doctor, he asks about it all,

He hears everything, "Weird, fantastic things"
The Messenger calls them: with their breasts
Swollen, their new babies abandoned, mothers

Among the Bacchantes nestled gazelles
And young wolves in their arms, and suckled them;
You might see a single one of them tear a fat calf

In two, still bellowing with fright, while others
Clawed heifers to pieces; ribs and hooves
Were strewn everywhere; blood-smeared scraps

Hung from the fir trees; furious bulls
Charged and then fell stumbling, pulled down
To be stripped of skin and flesh by screaming women . . .

And Pentheus listened. Flames burned in their hair,
Unnoticed; thick honey spurted from their wands;
And the snakes they wore like ribbons licked

Hot blood from their flushed necks: Pentheus
Was the man the people told . . . "weird things," like
A middle-class fantasy of release; and when even

The old men—bent Cadmus and Tiresias—dress up
In fawnskin and ivy, beating their wands on the ground,
Trying to carouse, it is Pentheus—down-to-earth,

Sober—who raises his voice in the name of dignity.
Being a psychiatrist, how could he attend to the Chorus's
     warning
Against "those who aspire" and "a tongue without reins"?

X. Dionysus As Psychiatrist

In a more hostile view, the psychiatrists
Are like Bacchus—the knowing smirk of his mask,
His patients, his confident guidance of passion,

And even his little jokes, as when the great palace
Is hit by lightning which blazes and stays,
Bouncing among the crumpling stone walls . . .

And through the burning rubble he comes,
With his soft ways picking along lightly
With a calm smile for the trembling Chorus

Who have fallen to the ground, bowing
In the un-Greek, Eastern way—What, Asian women,
He asks, Were you disturbed just now when Bacchus

Jostled the palace? He warns Pentheus to adjust,
To learn the ordinary man's humble sense of limits,
Violent limits, to the rational world. He cures

Pentheus of the grand delusion that the dark
Urgencies can be governed simply by the mind,
And the mind's will. He teaches Queen Agave to look

Up from her loom, up at the light, at her tall
Son's head impaled on the stiff spear clutched
In her own hand soiled with dirt and blood.

XI. Their Philistinism Considered

"Greek Tragedy" of course is the sort of thing
They like and like the idea of . . . though not "tragedy"
In the sense of newspapers. When a patient shot one of
      them,

People phoned in, many upset as though a deep,
Special rule had been abrogated, someone had gone too
      far.
The poor doctor, as described by the evening *Globe*,

Turned out to be a decent, conventional man (Doctors
For Peace, B'Nai Brith, numerous articles), almost
Carefully so, like Paul Valéry—or like Rex Morgan, M.D.,
  who,

In the same *Globe,* attends a concert with a longjawed
  woman.
First Panel: *"We're a little early for the concert!*
There's an art museum we can stroll through!" "I'd like

That, Dr. Morgan!" Second Panel: *"Outside the hospital,*
There's no need for such formality, Karen! Call me
By my first name!" "I'll feel a little awkward!"

Final Panel: *"Meanwhile . . ."* a black car pulls up
To City Hospital. . . . By the next day's *Globe,* the real
Doctor has died of gunshot wounds, while for smiling,
  wooden,

Masklike Rex and his companion the concert has passed,
Painlessly, offstage: *"This was a beautiful experience, Rex!"*
"I'm glad you enjoyed it! I have season tickets

And you're welcome to use them! I don't have
The opportunity to go to many of the concerts!"
Second Panel: *"You must be famished!"* And so Rex

And Karen go off to smile over a meal which will pass
Like music offstage, off to the mysterious pathos
Of their exclamation-marks, while in the final panel

"Meanwhile, In The Lobby At City Hospital"
A longjawed man paces furiously among
The lamps, magazines, tables and tubular chairs.

XII. Their Philistinism Dismissed

But after all—what "cultural life" and what
Furniture, what set of the face, would seem adequate
For those who supply medicine for misery?

After all, what they do is in a way a kind of art,
And what writers have to say about music, or painters'
Views about poetry, musicians' taste in pictures, all

Often are similarly hoked-up, dutiful, vulgar. After all,
They are not gods or heroes, nor even priests chosen
Apart from their own powers, but like artists are mere

Experts dependent on their own wisdom, their own arts:
Pilgrims in the world, journeymen, bourgeois savants,
Gallant seekers and persistent sons, doomed

To their cruel furniture and their season tickets
As to skimped meditations and waxen odes.
At first, Rex Morgan seems a perfect Pentheus—

But he smirks, he is imperturbable, he understates;
Understatement is the privilege of a god, we must
Choose, we must find out which way to see them:

Either the bland arrogance of the abrupt mountain god
Or the man of the town doing his best, we must not
Complain both that they are inhuman and too human.

XIII. Their Despair

I am quite sure that I have read somewhere
That the rate of suicide among psychiatrists
Is far higher than for any other profession.

There are many myths to explain such things, things
Which one reads and believes without believing
Any one significance for them—as in this case,

Which again reminds me of writers, who, I have read,
Drink and become alcoholics and die of alcoholism
In far greater numbers than other people.

Symmetry suggests one myth, or significance: the
    drinking
Of writers coming from too much concentration,
In solitude, upon feelings expressed

For or even about possibly indifferent people, people
Who are absent or perhaps dead, or unborn; the suicide
Of psychiatrists coming from too much attention,

In most intimate contact, concentrated upon the feelings
Of people toward whom one may feel indifferent,
People who are certain, sooner or later, to die . . .

Or people about whom they care too much, after all?
The significance of any life, of its misery and its end,
Is not absolute—that is the despair which

Underlies their good sense, recycling their garbage,
Voting, attending town-meetings, synagogues, churches,
Weddings, contingent gatherings of all kinds.

XIV. Their Speech, Compared With
Wisdom And Poetry

Terms of all kinds mellow with time, growing
Arbitrary and rich as we call this man "neurotic"
Or that man "a peacock." The lore of psychiatrists—

"Paranoid," "Anal" and so on, if they still use
Such terms—also passes into the status of old sayings:
Water thinner than blood or under bridges; bridges

Crossed in the future or burnt in the past. Or the terms
Of myth, the phrases that well up in my mind:
Two blind women and a blind little boy, running—

Easier to cut thin air into planks with a saw
And then drive nails into those planks of air,
Than to evade those three, the blind harriers,

The tireless blind women and the blind boy, pursuing
For long years of my life, for long centuries of time.
Concerning Justice, Fortune and Love I believe

That there may be wisdom, but no science and few terms:
Blind, and blinding, too. Hot in pursuit and flight,
Justice, Fortune and Love demand the arts

Of knowing and naming: and, yes, the psychiatrists, too,
Patiently naming them. But all in pursuit and flight, two
Blind women, tireless, and the blind little boy.

XV. A Footnote Concerning Psychiatry Itself

Having mentioned it, though it is not
My subject here, I will say only that one
Hopes it is good, and hopes that practicing it

The psychiatrists who are my subject here
Will respect the means, however pathetic,
That precede them; that they respect the patient's

Own previous efforts, strategies, civilizations—
Not only whatever it is that lets a man consciously
Desire girls of sixteen (or less) on the street,

And not embrace them, et cetera, but everything that was
There already: the restraints, and the other lawful
Old culture of wine, women, et cetera.

XVI. Generalizing, Just And Unjust

As far as one can generalize, only a few
Are not Jewish. Many, I have heard, grew up
As an only child. Among many general charges

Brought against them (smugness, obfuscation)
Is a hard, venal quality. In truth, they do differ
From most people in the special, tax-deductible status

Of their services, an enviable privilege which brings
Venality to the eye of the beholder, who feels
With some justice that if to soothe misery

Is a tax-deductible medical cost, then the lute-player,
Waitress, and actor also deserve to offer
Their services as tax-deductible; movies and TV

Should be tax-deductible . . . or nothing should;
Such cash matters perhaps lead psychiatrists
And others to buy what ought not to be sold: Seder

Services at hotels; skill at games from paid lessons;
Fast divorce; the winning side in a war seen
On TV like cowboys or football—*that* is how much

One can generalize: psychiatrists are as alike (and unlike)
As cowboys. In fact, they are stock characters like cowboys:
"Bette Davis, Claude Rains in *Now Voyager* (1942),

A sheltered spinster is brought out of her shell
By her psychiatrist" and "Steven Boyd, Jack Hawkins
In *The Third Secret* (1964), a psychoanalyst's

Daughter asks a patient to help her find her father's
Murderer." Like a cowboy, the only child roams
The lonely ranges and secret mesas of his genre.

XVII. Their Patients

As a rule, the patients I know do not pace
Furiously, nor scream, nor shoot doctors. For them,
To be a patient seems not altogether different

From one's interest in Anne Landers and her clients:
Her virtue of taking it all on, answering
Any question (artificial insemination by grandpa;

The barracuda of a girl who says that your glasses
Make you look square) and her virtue of saying,
Buster (or Dearie) stop complaining and do

What you want . . . and often that seems to be the point:
After the glassware from Design Research, after
A place on the Cape with Marimekko drapes,

The superlative radio and shoes, comes
The contingency tax—serious people, their capacity
For mere hedonism fills up, one seems to need

To perfect more complex ideas of desire,
To overcome altruism in the technical sense,
To learn to say no when you mean no and yes

When you mean yes, a standard of *cui bono,* a standard
Which, though it seems to be the inverse
Of more Spartan or Christian codes, is no less

Demanding in its call, inward in this case, to duty.
It suggests a kind of league of men and women
    dedicated
To their separate, inward duties, holding in common

Only the most general standard, or no standard
Other than valuing a sense of the conflict
Among standards, a league recalling in its mutual

Conflict and comfort the well-known fact that
    psychiatrists,
Too, are the patients of other psychiatrists,
Working dutifully—*cui bono*—at the inward standards.

XVIII. The Mad

Other patients are ill otherwise, and do
Scream and pace and kill or worse; and that
Should be recalled. Kit Smart, Hitler,

The contemporary poets of lunacy—none of them
Helps me to think of the mad otherwise
Than in cliches too broad, the maenads

And wild-eyed killers of the movies . . .
But perhaps lunacy feels something like a cliche,
A desperate or sweet yielding to some broad,

Mechanical simplification, a dispersal
Of the unbearable into its crude fragments,
The distraction of a repeated gesture

Or a compulsively hummed tune. Maybe
It is not utterly different from chewing
At one's fingernails. For the psychiatrists

It must come to seem ordinary, its causes
And the causes of its relief, after all,
No matter how remote and intricate, are no

Stranger than life itself, which was born or caused
Itself, once, as a kind of odor, a faint wreath
Brewing where the radiant light from billions

Of miles off strikes a faint broth from water
Standing in rock; life born from the egg
Of rock, and the egglike rock of death

Are no more strange than this other life
Which we name after the moon, lunatic
Other-life . . . housed, for the lucky ones,

In McLean's Hospital with its elegant,
Prep-school atmosphere. When my friend
Went in, we both tried to joke: "Karen," I said,

"You must be crazy to spend money and time
In this place"—she gained weight,
Made a chess-board, had a room-mate

Who introduced herself as the Virgin Mary,
Referred to another patient: "Well, she must
Be an interesting person, if she's in here."

XIX. Peroration, Defining Happiness

"I know not how it is, but certainly I
Have never been more tired with any reading
Than with dissertations upon happiness,

Which seems not only to elude inquiry,
But to cast unmerciful loads of clay
And sand and husks and stubble

Along the high-road of the inquirer.
Even sound writers talk mostly in a drawling
And dreaming way about it. He,

Who hath given the best definition
Of most things, hath given but an imperfect one,
Here, informing us that a happy life

Is one without impediment to virtue. . . .
In fact, hardly anything which we receive
For truth is really and entirely so,

Let it appear plain as it may, and let
Its appeal be not only to the understanding,
But to the senses; for our words do not follow

The senses exactly; and it is by words
We receive truth and express it."
So says Walter Savage Landor in his Imaginary

Conversation between Sir Philip Sidney
And Fulke Greville, Lord Brooke, all three,
In a sense, my own psychiatrists, shrinking

The sense of contingency and confusion
Itself to a few terms I can quote, ponder
Or type: the idea of wisdom, itself, shrinks.

XX. Peroration, Concerning Genius

As to my own concerns, it seems odd, given
The ideas many of us have about art,
That so many writers, makers of films,

Artists, all suitors of excellence and their own
Genius, should consult psychiatrists, willing
To risk that the doctor in curing

The sickness should smooth away the cicatrice
Of genius, too. But it is all bosh, the false
Link between genius and sickness,

Except perhaps as they were linked
By the Old Man, addressing his class
On the first day: *"I know why you are here.*

You are here to laugh. You have heard of a crazy
Old man who believes that Robert Bridges
Was a good poet; who believes that Fulke

Greville was a great poet, greater than Philip
Sidney; who believes that Shakespeare's Sonnets
Are not all that they are cracked up to be.... Well,

I will tell you something: I will tell you
What this course is about. Sometime in the middle
Of the Eighteenth Century, along with the rise

Of capitalism and scientific method, the logical
Foundations of Western thought decayed and fell apart.
When they fell apart, poets were left

With emotions and experiences, and with no way
To examine them. At this time, poets and men
Of genius began to go mad. Gray went mad. Collins

Went mad. Kit Smart was mad. William Blake surely
Was a madman. Coleridge was a drug addict, with severe
Depression. My friend Hart Crane died mad. My friend

Ezra Pound is mad. But you will not go mad; you will
      grow up
To become happy, sentimental old college professors,
Because they were men of genius, and you

Are not; and the ideas which were vital
To them are mere amusement to you. I will not
Go mad, because I have understood those ideas. . . ."

He drank wine and smoked his pipe more than he
      should;
In the end his doctors in order to prolong life
Were forced to cut away most of his tongue.

That was their business. As far as he was concerned
Suffering was life's penalty; wisdom armed one
Against madness; speech was temporary; poetry was truth.

XXI. Conclusion

Essaying to distinguish these men and women,
Who try to give medicine for misery,
From the rest of us, I find I have failed

To discover what essential statement could be made
About psychiatrists that would not apply
To all human beings, or what statement

About all human beings would not apply
Equally to psychiatrists. They, too,
Consult psychiatrists. They try tentatively

To understand, to find healing speech. They work
For truth and for money. They are contingent . . .
They talk and talk . . . they are, in the words

Of a lute-player I met once who despised them,
"Into machines" . . . all true of all, so that it seems
That "psychiatrist" is a synonym for "human being,"

Even in their prosperity which is perhaps
Like their contingency merely more vivid than that
Of lutanists, opticians, poets—all into

Truth, into music, into yearning, suffering,
Into elegant machines and luxuries, with caroling
And kisses, with soft rich cloth and polished

Substances, with cash, tennis and fine electronics,
Liberty of lush and reverend places—goods
And money in their contingency and spiritual

Grace evoke the way we are all psychiatrists,
All fumbling at so many millions of miles
Per minute and so many dollars per hour

Through the exploding or collapsing spaces
Between stars, saying what we can.

AN EXPLANATION OF AMERICA

(1979)

Lair

Inexhaustible, delicate, as if
Without source or medium, daylight
Undoes the mind; the infinite,

Empty actual is too bright,
Scattering to where the road
Whispers, through a mile of woods . . .

Later, how quiet the house is:
Dusk-like and refined,
The sweet Phoebe-note

Piercing from the trees;
The calm globe of the morning,
Things to read or to write

Ranged on a table; the brain
A dark, stubborn current that breathes
Blood, a deaf wadding,

The hands feeding it paper
And sensations of wood or metal
On its own terms. Trying to read

I persist a while, finish the recognition
By my breath of a dead giant's breath—
Stayed by the space of a rhythm,

Witnessing the blue gulf of the air.

An Explanation Of America

A POEM TO MY DAUGHTER

Part One:

Its Many Fragments

I. Prologue: You

As though explaining the idea of dancing
Or the idea of some other thing
Which everyone has known a little about
Since they were children, which children learn
    themselves
With no explaining, but which children like
Sometimes to hear the explanations of,
I want to tell you something about our country,
Or my idea of it: explaining it
If not to you, to my idea of you.

Dancing is the expression by the body
Of how the soul and brain respond to music—
And yes, not only to the sensual, God-like,
Varying repetitions which we love
But also, I admit it, to harmony, too:
As of a group. But what the Brownies did
Gathered inside a church the other day

(Except for one flushed Leader, smiling and skipping
With shoes off through the dance) was Close Drill:
    frowning,
The children shuffled anxiously at command
Through the home-stitched formations of the Square
    Dance.
Chewing your nails, you couldn't get it straight.
Another Leader, with her face exalted
By something like a passion after order,
Was roughly steering by the shoulders, each
In turn, two victims: brilliant, incompetent you;
And a tight, humiliated blonde, her daughter.
But before going on about groups, leaders,
Churches and such, I think I want to try
To explain you. Countries and people of course
Cannot be known or told in final terms . . .
But can be, in the comic, halting way
Of parents, explained: as Death and Government are.
I don't mean merely to *pretend* to write
To you, yet don't mean either to pretend
To say only what you might want to hear.
I mean to write to my idea of you,
And not expecting you to read a word . . .
Though you are better at understanding words
Than most people I know. You understand
An Old Man's Winter Night. And I believe,
Compulsive explainer that I am, and you
Being who you are, that if I felt the need
To make some smart, professor-ish crack about
Walt Whitman, the Internment Camps, or *Playboy*

I could, if necessary, explain it to you,
Who, writing under the name of "Karen Owens,"
Began your "Essay On Kids": *"In my opinion,*
We 'tots' are truly in the 'prime of life,'
Of all creatures on earth, or other planets
Should there be life on such."

                                    In games and plays,
You like to be the Bad Guy, Clown or Dragon,
Not Mother or The Princess. Your favorite creature
Is the Owl, the topic of another "Essay."
Garrulous, prosy, good at spelling and fond
Of punctuation, you cannot form two letters
Alike or on a line. You suck your thumb
And have other infantile traits, although
A student interviewing "tots" from five
To eight for her psychology project found,
Scaling results, that your ideas of God
And of your dreams were those of an adult.
Though I should never tell you that (or this)
It occurs to me, thinking of Chaplin, Twain
And others—thinking of owls, the sacred bird
Of Athens and Athene—that it is not
A type (the solitary flights at night;
The dreams mature, the spirit infantile)
Which America has always known to prize.
—Not that I mean to class you with the great
At your age, but that the celebrated examples
(Ted Williams comes to mind) recall your face,
The soft long lashes behind the owlish glasses
Which you selected over "cuter" frames:

That softness—feathery, protective, inward—
Muffling the quickness of the raptor's eye,
The gaze of liberty and independence
Uneasy in groups and making groups uneasy.

II. From the Surface

A country is the things it wants to see.
If so, some part of me, though I do not,
Must want to see these things—as if to say:

"I want to see the calf with two heads suckle;
I want to see the image of a woman
In rapid sequence of transparencies
Projected on a bright flat surface, conveying
The full illusion and effect of motion,
In vast, varying scale, with varying focus,
Swallow the image of her partner's penis.
I want to see enormous colored pictures
Of people with impossible complexions,
Dressed, often, in flamboyant clothes, along
The roads and fastened to the larger buildings.
I want to see men playing games with balls.
I want to see new cars; I want to see
Faces of people, famous, or in times
Of great emotion, or both; and above all,
It seems, I want to see the anthropomorphic
Animals drawn for children, as represented
By people in smiling masks and huge costumes.
I want to shake their hands. I want to see
Cars crashing; cards with a collie or a pipe
And slippers, dry flies, mallards and tennis rackets—
Two people kissing for Valentine, and then
A nicky-nacky design, a little puppy
Begging for me to like the person who mailed it."
In Mexico, I suppose they want to see

The Eyes of God, and dogs and ponies coupling
With women, skeletons in hats and skirts,
Dishwashers, plutocrats humiliated,
Clark Gable, flashy bauhaus buildings, pistols.
It always is disturbing, what a country
Of people want to see. . . . In England once,
A country that I like, between two Terms,
In Oxford, I saw a traveling carnival
And fair with Morris dancers, and a woman
Down in a shallow pit—bored-looking, with bored
And overfed, drugged-looking brown rats lolling
Around her white bare body where it was chained
Among them: sluggish, in a furtive tent.

And that was something, like the Morris dance,
Which an American would neither want
To see, nor think of hiding, which helps to prove
That after all these countries do exist,
All of us sensing what we want to see
Whether we want it separately, or not.

But beyond the kinds of ball or billboard, or what
The woman must undergo, are other proofs,
Suggesting that all countries are the same:
And that the awful, trivial, and atrocious
(Those "forms receptive, featureless and vast")
Are what all peoples want to see and hide,
Are similar everywhere, and every year
Take forms that are increasingly the same,
Time and *Der Spiegel,* Chile and Chicago,

All coming to one thing, whether sinister
Or bland as a Christmas card from "Unicef."

What do I want for you to see? I want—
Beyond the states and corporations, each
Hiding and showing after their kind the forms
Of their atrocities, beyond their power
For evil—the greater evil in ourselves,
And greater images more vast than *Time*.
I want for you to see the things I see
And more, Colonial Diners, Disney, films
Of concentration camps, the napalmed child
Trotting through famous newsfilm in her diaper
And tattered flaps of skin, *Deep Throat*, the rest.

I want our country like a common dream
To be between us in what we want to see—
Not that I want for you to have to see
Atrocity itself, or that its image
Is harmless. I mean the way we need to see
With shared, imperfect memory: the quiet
Of tourists shuffling with their different awes
Through well-kept Rushmore, Chiswick House, or Belsen;
"Lest we forget" and its half-forgotten aura.
I want for you to see a "hippie restaurant"
And the rock valley where a hundred settlers
Were massacred by other settlers, dressed
As Indians—like the Boston tea-tax rioters
Or like the college kids who work for Disney,
Showing the people what they want to see.

III. Local Politics

And so the things the country wants to see
Are like a nest made out of circumstance;
And when, as in the great old sermon "The Eagle
Stirreth Her Nest," God like a nesting eagle
Pulls out a little of the plush around us
And lets the thorns of trial, and the bramble,
Stick through and scrape and threaten the fledgling soul,
We see that that construction of thorn and bramble
Is like a cage: the tight and sheltering cage
Of Law and circumstance, scraping through the plush
Like death—whenever the eagle stirreth her nest,
The body with its bony cage of law
And politics, the thorn of death and taxes.

You, rich in rhetoric and indignation,
The jailbird-lawyer of the Hunnewell School,
Come home from some small, wicked parliament
To elaborate a new theme: forceful topics
Touching the sheeplike, piggish ways of that tyrant
And sycophantic lout, the Majority.
The two lame cheers for democracy that I
Borrow and try to pass to you ("It is
The worst of all the forms of government,
Except for all the others"—Winston Churchill)
You brush aside: Political Science bores you,
You prefer the truth, and with a Jesuit firmness
Return to your slogan: "Voting *is not* fair."
I have another saw that I can scrape
For you, out of the hoard of antique hardware,

Cliches and Great Ideas, quaintly-toothed
Black ironwork that we heap about our young:
Voting is one of the *"necessary evils."*
Avoid all groups and institutions, they
Are necessary evils: necessary
Unto the general Happiness and Safety,
And evil because they are deficient in being.
Such is the hardware; and somewhere in between
The avoidance and the evil necessity
We each conclude a contract with the Beast.

America is, as Malcolm X once said,
A prison. And that the world and all its parts
Are also prisons (Chile, the Hunnewell School,
One's own deficient being, each prison after
Its own degree and kind), does not diminish
Anything that he meant about his country:
When the Dan Ryan Expressway in Chicago
Was flooded, "Black youths" who the paper said
Pillaged the stranded motorists like beached whales
Were rioting prisoners ... a weight of lead
Sealed in their hearts was lighter for some minutes
Amid the riot.
                        Living inside a prison,
Within its many other prisons, what
Should one aspire to be? a kind of chaplain?
But chaplains, I have heard, are often powers,
Political, within their prisons, patrons
And mediators between the frightened groups:
Blue People, Gray People, and their constricting fears,
The mutual circumstance of ward and warder.

No kind of chaplain ever will mediate
Among the conquering, crazed immigrants
Of El Camino and the Bergen Mall,
The Jews who dream up the cowboy films, the Blacks
Who dream the music, the people who dream the cars
And ways of voting, the Japanese and Basques
Each claiming a special sense of humor, as do
Armenian photo-engravers, and the people
Who dream the saws: *"You cannot let men live
Like pigs, and make them freemen, it is not safe,"*
The people who dream up the new diseases
For use in warfare, the people who design
New shapes of pants, and sandwiches sumptuous
Beyond the dreams of innocent Europe: crazed
As carpet-bombing or the Berlin Airlift—
Crazed immigrants and prisoners, rioting
Or else, alone as in the secrecy
Of a narrow bunk or cell, whittling or painting
Some desperate weapon or crude work of art:
A spoon honed to a dagger or a bauble,
A pistol molded from a cake of soap,
A fumbling poem or a lurid picture
Urgent and sentimental as a tattoo. . . .
The Dorians, too, were conquering immigrants,
And hemmed in by their own anarchic spirits
And new peninsula, they too resorted
To invented institutions, and the vote,
With a spirit nearly comic, and in fear.

The plural-headed Empire, manifold
Beyond my outrage or my admiration,
Is like a prison which I leave to you
(And like a shelter)—where the people vote,
And where the threats of riot and oppression
Inspire the inmates as they whittle, scribble,
Jockey for places in the choir, or smile
Passing out books on weekdays.
                                    On the radio,
The FM station that plays "All Country and Western"
Startled me, when I hit its button one day,
With a voice—inexplicable and earnest—
In Vietnamese or Chinese, lecturing
Or selling, or something someone wanted broadcast,
A paid political announcement, perhaps. . . .
"All politics is local politics"
Said Mayor Daley (in pentameter):
And this then is the locus where we vote,
Prisonyard fulcrum of knowledge, fear and work—
Nest where an Eagle balances and screams,
The wild bird with its hardware in its claws.

IV. Countries and Explanations

Gogol explains his country as a troika:
"What Russian doesn't like fast driving," he says,
"Exalted by the dark pines flashing past
Like smoke? . . . And you, my Russia—racing on
To God knows where in an endless, manic blur,
Like the most birdlike troika ever made
By a Russian peasant with an axe and chisel:
No screws, no metal—thundering past the milestones
Like spots before your eyes; and spreading out
Evenly over half the world! . . . A blur;
A jingling of bells, and rattling bridges; the road
Smokes under your wheels as everything falls behind;
The horses take fire, barely touching the earth;
And you become entirely a flow of air,
Inspired by God—Russia, where do you fly?"

She doesn't answer. The air is torn to shreds
And becomes mere wind behind the flying troika;
And the other countries, with nervous glances sideways-
So many pedestrians, startled at the curb—
Step to one side: astonished at the speed
And eloquence of Gogol's explanation,
His country thundering madly down the highway. . . .

Somebody might explain a troubled time
By saying, "It's because they killed the railroads":
Because a child who hears a whistle at night
Can hear it drawing closer to the bed
And further in a line, along a vein,

While highways murmuring in the night are like
A restless river, grown unpredictable
A way that rivers don't.
                                And yet the shadows
From headlights as they circled my bedroom walls
Have given me comfort too, the lights and whistle
Like two different sentimental songs
At night. And though the cars and highways do stifle
The downtowns and their sweet co-operation
(The City Bakery, the Paramount, the stores)
I love a car—a car, I guess, is like
One's personality, corrupt and selfish,
Full of hypnotic petty pains and joys,
While riding on a train is like the mind,
The separate reveries, the communal rhythm
Of motion in a line, along a vein. . . .

The communal speed of trains and happy freedom
In a car are like the troika: speed making plain
The great size of its place, the exhilaration
Of change which the size evokes—the schedules,
     pillows
And porters on the train, the thrill of wit
And aggression in a car, choosing a lane—
Yet some day, tamed and seasoned, our machines
Might make plain that America is a country:
Another country like others with their myths
Of their uniqueness, Tara and Golden Peru
And headlong Mother Russia or Colombia,
Finlandia and the Cowboy's Prayer, and even

Quiet Helvetia; each place a country
With myths and anthems and its heroic name.

And motion would be a place, and who knows, you
May live there in the famous national "love
Of speed" as though in some small town where children
Walk past their surnames in the churchyard, you
At home among the murmur of that place
Unthinkable for me, but for the children
Of that place comforting as an iceman's horse.

Because as all things have their explanations,
True or false, all can come to seem domestic.
The brick mills of New England on their rivers
Are *brooding, classic*; the Iron Horse is quaint,
Steel oildrums, musical; and the ugly suburban
"Villas" of London, Victorian Levittowns,
Have come to be civilized and urbane.

And so, although a famous wanderer
Defines a nation, "The same people living
In the same place," by such strange transformations
Of time the motion from place to place itself
May come to be the place we have in common.
The regions and their ways—like Northern Michigan
And its Rutabaga Pasties, or Union City
With its Cuban and Armenian churches—will be
As though Officially Protected Species.
The Shopping Center itself will be as precious
And quaint as is the threadmill now converted
Into a quaint and high-class shopping center.

For *place,* itself, is always a kind of motion,
A part of it artificial and preserved,
And a part born in a blur of loss and change—
All places in motion from where we thought they were,
Boston before it was Irish or Italian,
Harlem and Long Branch before we ever knew
That they were beautiful, and when they were:
Our nation, mellowing to another country
Of different people living in different places.

Part Two:

Its Great Emptiness

I. A Love of Death

Imagine a child from Virginia or New Hampshire
Alone on the prairie eighty years ago
Or more, one afternoon—the shaggy pelt
Of grasses, for the first time in that child's life,
Flowing for miles. Imagine the moving shadow
Of a cloud far off across that shadeless ocean,
The obliterating strangeness like a tide
That pulls or empties the bubble of the child's
Imaginary heart. No hills, no trees.

The child's heart lightens, tending like a bubble
Towards the currents of the grass and sky,
The pure potential of the clear blank spaces.

Or, imagine the child in a draw that holds a garden
Cupped from the limitless motion of the prairie,
Head resting against a pumpkin, in evening sun.
Ground-cherry bushes grow along the furrows,

The fruit red under its papery, moth-shaped sheath.
Grasshoppers tumble among the vines, as large
As dragons in the crumbs of pale dry earth.
The ground is warm to the child's cheek, and the wind
Is a humming sound in the grass above the draw,
Rippling the shadows of the red-green blades.
The bubble of the child's heart melts a little,
Because the quiet of that air and earth
Is like the shadow of a peaceful death—
Limitless and potential, a kind of space
Where one dissolves to become a part of something
Entire . . . whether of sun and air, or goodness
And knowledge, it does not matter to the child.

Dissolved among the particles of the garden
Or into the motion of the grass and air,
Imagine the child happy to be a thing.

Imagine, then, that on that same wide prairie
Some people are threshing in the terrible heat
With horses and machines, cutting bands
And shoveling amid the clatter of the threshers,
The chaff in prickly clouds and the naked sun
Burning as if it could set the chaff on fire.
Imagine that the people are Swedes or Germans,
Some of them resting pressed against the strawstacks,
Trying to get the meager shade.
                                            A man,
A tramp, comes laboring across the stubble
Like a mirage against that blank horizon,
Laboring in his torn shoes toward the tall

Mirage-like images of the tilted threshers
Clattering in the heat. Because the Swedes
Or Germans have no beer, or else because
They cannot speak his language properly,
Or for some reason one cannot imagine,
The man climbs up on a thresher and cuts bands
A minute or two, then waves to one of the people,
A young girl or a child, and jumps head-first
Into the sucking mouth of the machine,
Where he is wedged and beat and cut to pieces—
While the people shout and run in the clouds of chaff,
Like lost mirages on the pelt of prairie.

The obliterating strangeness and the spaces
Are as hard to imagine as the love of death . . .
Which is the love of an entire strangeness,
The contagious blankness of a quiet plain.
Imagine that a man, who had seen a prairie,
Should write a poem about a Dark or Shadow
That seemed to be both his, and the prairie's—as if
The shadow proved that he was not a man,
But something that lived in quiet, like the grass.
Imagine that the man who writes that poem,
Stunned by the loneliness of that wide pelt,
Should prove to himself that he was like a shadow
Or like an animal living in the dark.

In the dark proof he finds in his poem, the man
Might come to think of himself as the very prairie,
The sod itself, not lonely, and immune to death.

None of this happens precisely as I try
To imagine that it does, in the empty plains,
And yet it happens in the imagination
Of part of the country: not in any place
More than another, on the map, but like
A place, where you and I have never been
And need to try imagining—like a prairie
Where immigrants, in the obliterating strangeness,
Thirst for the wide contagion of the shadow
Or prairie—where you and I, with our other ways,
More like the cities or the hills or trees,
Less like the clear blank spaces with their potential,
Are like strangers in a place we must imagine.

II. Bad Dreams

In a way, every stranger must imagine
The place where he finds himself—as shrewd Odysseus
Was able to imagine, as he wandered,
The ways and perils of a foreign place:
Making his goal, not knowing the real place,
But his survival, and his progress home.
And everyone has felt it—foreign ground,
With its demand on the imagination
Like the strange gaze of the cattle of the Sun—
Unless one is an angel, or a hick,
A tribesman who never made his wander-year.

People who must, like immigrants or nomads,
Live always in imaginary places
Think of some past or word to fill a blank—
The encampment at the Pole or at the Summit;
Comanches in Los Angeles; the Jews
Of Russia or Romania, who lived
In Israel before it was a place or thought,
But a pure, memorized word which they knew better
Than their own hands.
                              And at the best such people,
However desperate, have a lightness of heart
That comes to the mind alert among its reasons,
A sense of the arbitrariness of the senses:
Blank snow subordinate to the textbook North.
Like tribesmen living in a real place,
With their games, jokes or gossip, a love of skill

And commerce, they keep from loving the blank of death.
But there are perils in living always in vision—
Always inventing entire whatever paves
Or animates the innocent sand or snow
Of a mere locale. What if the place itself
Should seem a blank, as in a country huge
And open and potential? . . . the blank enlarges,
And swelling in concentric gusts of quiet
Absorbs the imagination in a cloud
Of quiet, as smoke disperses through a mist,
A vague chimera that engulfs the breath.

That quiet leads me to a stranger's dread
Of the place frightened settlers might invent:
The customs of the people there, the tongues
They speak, and what they have to drink, the things
That they imagine, might falter in such a place,
Or be too few; and men would live like Cyclopes,
"With neither assemblies nor any settled customs"—
Or Laestrygonians who consume their kind
And see a stranger as his meat and marrow,
And have no cities or cultivated farms.

A man who eats the lotus of his prairie
Or shadow—consumed by his desire for darkness
Till the mind seems itself a dreamy marrow—
Is like those creatures of a traveler's nightmare.
Even his sentiments about the deer,
Or grass, recall man-eating Polyphemus:
Who, when he cracks like a movie Nazi, sheds

Real tears, making a sentimental speech
To his pet ram.
                          In place of settled customs,
Such a man might set up a brazen calf,
Or join a movement, fanatical, to spite
The spirit of assembly, or of words—
To drown that chatter and gossip, and become
Sure, like machines and animals and the earth.

Such a man—neither a Greek adventurer
With his pragmatic gods, nor an Indian,
Nor Jew—would worship, not an earth or past
Or word, but something immanent, like a shadow
Perhaps he was once a Protestant, with a God
Whose hand was in every berry, insect, cloud:
Not in the Indian way, but as one hand,
Immanent, above that berry and its name.

And when that hand came to him as a prairie
He beheld pure space as if it were a god,
Or as a devil. And if he lost that hand,
Why wouldn't he—in his loneliness and love
Of thinking nothing—grow eager to lose himself
Among a brazen crowd, as in a calf,
A certain landscape, or a bird?
                                                    Or say
That he sets out upon that empty plain
Immanent with a quiet beyond all thought
Or words, and that he settles on that ground
Of trial, to invent a mystic home—
And then discovers people there, engaged

Upon their commerce or their gossip, at home
Or wandering as in an actual place,
Attending to their ordinary business:
The ordinary passion to bring death
For gain or glory, as Odysseus
Might feel, would be augmented and inflamed
By the harsh passion of a settler; and so,
Why wouldn't he bring his death to Indians
Or Jews, or Greeks who stop for food and water,
To bustle and jabber on his tangled plain?

But my nightmare is not the one you have
To fear, exactly, and if the Cyclops comes
(Lumbering, hungry, unreasoning, drunk or blind)
He may come gently, without commotion, cloaked
More in the manner—as in poems by Auden—
Of a disquieting nurse, an official form
With its inquiry, than of my bad dreams.

For I am father and mother of my man
(Who is no man, but something I imagined,
Or a kind of word for something that I fear),
And perhaps I am his child, too: choosing to be
Myself explaining him, or him—like people
Who have mixed blood, and might feel free to choose
To be themselves as Indians, or Cowboys . . .
With their high cheekbones, blue eyes, and iron hair.
And you and I, who have no Indian blood
(Or Cowboy blood, assuming such a thing)
Imagine two sides of people—with their blood,
A place, a climate, their circumstances fixed

As bounds for choice or for imagination—
Hardly free: the takers ready to kill
To take the theater of their imagined home,
Still half imaginary; the defenders
At home in places that became the more
Imaginary as the white ones took
Tobacco; taught scalping; introduced the horse.

And even Malcolm X, who changed his name
So many times, whom we remember now
Most by that one name which still means "unknown"-
Possibly "free"—must, with his many names
And his red hair, have needed to consider
The kinds of arbitrariness and choice:
The arbitrariness of the blood and senses
Compared to the poles and summits of our choosing,
The textbook "Indian," "American" or "blood" . . .
The accumulating prison of the past
That pulls us towards a body and a place.

My imaginary man is in that prison,
Though he thinks only of the feral earth,
Making himself less free.
                                        Then let him rest;
And think instead of the European poets
Posed thoughtfully with cigarettes or scarves,
As photographed for a fascist anthology
Of forty years ago, above their verses
About a landscape, tribe, or mystic shadow:
Caught in the prison of their country's earth
Or its Romantic potential, born of death

Or of a pure idea. *". . .Italy*
(Germany, Russia, America, Romania)
Had never really been a country," a book
Might say, explaining something.

                                What I want
And want for you is not a mystic home
But something—if it must be imaginary—
Chosen from life, and useful. Nietzsche says
We should admire the traffickers and nomads

"Who have that freedom of the mind and soul
Which mankind learns from frequent changes of place,
Climate and customs, new neighbors and oppressors."

Americans, we choose to see ourselves
As here, yet not here yet—as if a Roman
In mid-Rome should inquire the way to Rome.
Like Jews or Indians, roving on the plains
Of places taken from us, or imagined,
We accumulate the customs, music, words
Of different climates, neighbors and oppressors,
Making encampment in the sand or snow.

III. Horace, Epistulæ I, xvi

The poet Horace, writing to a friend
About his Sabine farm and other matters,
Implies his answer about aspiration
Within the prison of empire or republic:

"Dear Quinctius:
                    I'll tell you a little about
My farm—in case you ever happen to wonder
About the place: as, what I make in grain,
Or if I'm getting rich on olives, apples,
Timber or pasture.
                       There are hills, unbroken
Except for one soft valley, cut at an angle
That sweetens the climate, because it takes the sun
All morning on its right slope, until the left
Has its turn, warming as the sun drives past
All afternoon. You'd like it here: the plums
And low-bush berries are ripe; and where my cows
Fill up on acorns and ilex-berries a lush
Canopy of shade gives pleasure to their master.
The green is deep, so deep you'd say Tarentum
Had somehow nestled closer, to be near Rome.

There is a spring, fit for a famous river
(The Hebrus winds through Thrace no colder or purer),
Useful for healing stomach-aches and head-aches.
And here I keep myself, and the place keeps me—
A precious good, believe it, Quinctius—
In health and sweetness through September's heat.

You of course live in the way that is truly right,
If you've been careful to remain the man
That we all see in you. We here in Rome
Talk of you, always, as 'happy' ... there is the fear,
Of course, that one might listen too much to others,
Think what they see, and strive to be that thing,
And lose by slow degrees that inward man
Others first noticed—as though, if over and over
Everyone tells you you're in marvelous health,
You might towards dinner-time, when a latent fever
Falls on you, try for a long while to disguise it,
Until the trembling rattles your food-smeared hands.
It's foolishness to camouflage our sores.

Take 'recognition'—what if someone writes
A speech about your service to your country,
Telling for your attentive ears the roll
Of all your victories by land or sea,
With choice quotations, dignified periods,
And skillful terms, all in the second person,
As in citations for honorary degrees:
'Only a mind beyond our human powers
Could judge if your great love for Rome exceeds,
Or is exceeded by, Rome's need for you.'

—You'd find it thrilling, but inappropriate
For anyone alive, except Augustus.

And yet if someone calls me 'wise' or 'flawless'
Must one protest? I like to be told I'm right,
And brilliant, as much as any other man.

The trouble is, the people who give out
The recognition, compliments, degrees
Can take them back tomorrow, if they choose;
The committee or electorate decide
You can't sit in the Senate, or have the Prize—
'Sorry, but isn't that ours, that you nearly took?'
What can I do, but shuffle sadly off?
If the same people scream that I'm a crook
Who'd strangle my father for money to buy a drink,
Should I turn white with pain and humiliation?
If prizes and insults from outside have much power
To hurt or give joy, something is sick inside.

Who is 'the good man'?
                          Many people would answer,
'He is the man who never breaks the law
Or violates our codes. His judgment is sound.
He is the man whose word is as his bond.
If such a man agrees to be your witness,
Your case is won.'
                          And yet this very man,
If you ask his family, or the people who know him,
Is like a rotten egg in its flawless shell.
And if a slave or prisoner should say
'I never steal; I never try to escape,'
My answer is, 'You have your just rewards:
No beatings; no solitary; and your food.'
'I have not killed.' 'You won't be crucified.'
'But haven't I shown that I am good, and honest?'

To this, my country neighbor would shake his head
And sigh: 'Ah no! The wolf himself is wary
Recause he fears the pit, as hawks the snare
Or pike the hook. Some folk hate vice for love
Of the good: you're merely afraid of guards and crosses.'

Apply that peasant wisdom to that 'good man'
Of forum and tribunal, who in the temple
Calls loudly on 'Father Janus' or 'Apollo'
But in an undertone implores, 'Laverna,
Goddess of thieves, O Fair One, grant me, please,
That I get away with it, let me pass as upright,
Cover my sins with darkness, my lies with clouds.'

When a man stoops to pluck at the coin some boys
Of Rome have soldered to the street, I think
That just then he is no more free than any
Prisoner, or slave; it seems that someone who wants
Too much to get things is also someone who fears,
And living in that fear cannot be free.
A man has thrown away his weapons, has quit
The struggle for virtue, who is always busy
Filling his wants, getting things, making hay—
Weaponless and defenseless as a captive.

When you have got a captive, you never kill him
If you can sell him for a slave; this man
Truly will make a good slave: persevering,
Ambitious, eager to please—as ploughman, or
    shepherd,

Or trader plying your goods at sea all winter,
Or helping to carry fodder at the farm. . . .
The truly good, and wise man has more courage;
And if need be, will find the freedom to say,
As in the *Bacchae* of Euripides:

King Pentheus, Lord of Thebes, what will you force me
To suffer at your hands?
>   *I will take your goods.*

You mean my cattle, furniture, cloth and plate?
Then you may have them.
>   *I will put you, chained,*
Into my prison, under a cruel guard.

Then God himself, the moment that I choose,
Will set me free. . . .

I think that what this means is: 'I will die.'

Death is the chalk-line towards which all things race."

IV. Filling the Blank

Odd, that the poet who seems so complacent
About his acorns and his cold pure water,
Writing from his retreat just out of Rome,
Should seem to end with a different love of death
From that of someone on a mystic plain—
But still, with love of death. "... A rather short man,"
He calls himself, "and prematurely gray,
Who liked to sit in the sun; a freedman's child
Who spread his wings too wide for that frail nest
And yet found favor, in both war and peace,
With powerful men. Tell them I lost my temper
Easily, but was easily appeased,
My book—and if they chance to ask my age
Say, I completed my forty-fourth December
In the first year that Lepidus was Consul."

I think that what the poet meant was this:
That freedom, even in a free Republic,
Rests ultimately on the right to die.
And though he's careful to say that Quinctius,
The public man able to act for good
And help his fellow-Romans, lives the life
That truly is the best, he's also careful
To separate their fortunes and their places,
And to appreciate his own: his health,
His cows and acorns and his healing spring,
His circle—*"We here in Rome"*—for friends and gossip.

It would be too complacent to build a nest
Between one's fatalism and one's pleasures—
With death at one side, a sweet farm at the other,
Keeping the thorns of government away. . . .

Horace's father, who had been a slave,
Engaged in some small business near Venusia;
And like a Jewish or Armenian merchant
Who does well in America, he sent
His son to Rome's best schools, and then to Athens
(It's hard to keep from thinking "as to Harvard")
To study, with the sons of gentlemen
And politicians, the higher arts most useful
To citizens of a Republic: math;
Philosophy; rhetoric in all its branches.

One March, when Horace, not quite twenty-one,
Was still at Athens, Julius Caesar died,
And the Roman world was split by civil war.

When Brutus came to Athens late that summer
On his way to Asia Minor—"half-mystical,
Wholly romantic Brutus"—Horace quit school
To follow Brutus to Asia, bearing the title
Or brevet-commission *tribunus militum,*
And served on the staff of the patriot-assassin.

Time passed; the father died; the property
And business were lost, or confiscated.
The son saw action at Philippi, where,
Along with other enthusiastic students
(Cicero's son among them), and tens of thousands

In the two largest armies of Roman soldiers
Ever to fight with one another, he shared
In the republican army's final rout
By Antony and Octavian.

                             Plutarch says
That Brutus, just before he killed himself,
Speaking in Greek to an old fellow-student,
Said that although he was angry for his country
He was deeply happy for himself—because
His virtue and his repute for virtue were founded
In a way none of the conquerors could hope,
For all their arms and riches, to emulate;
Nor could they hinder posterity from knowing,
And saying, that they were unjust and wicked men
Who had destroyed justice and the Republic,
Usurping a power to which they had no right.

The corpse of Brutus was found by Antony,
And he commanded the richest purple mantle
In his possession to be thrown over it,
And afterwards, the mantle being stolen,
He found the thief and had him put to death;
The ashes of Brutus he sent back to Rome,
To be received with honor by the mourners.

Horace came back to Rome a pardoned rebel
In his late twenties, without cash or prospects,
Having stretched out his wings too far beyond
The frail nest of his freedman father's hopes,
As he has written.

                        When he was thirty-five,

He published some poems which some people praised,
And so through Vergil he met the Roman knight
And good friend of Augustus, called Maecenas,
Who befriended him, and gave him the Sabine farm;
And in that place, and in the highest circles
In Rome itself, he spent his time, and wrote.

Since aspirations need not (some say, should not)
Be likely, should I wish for you to be
A hero, like Brutus—who at the finish-line
Declared himself to be a happy man?
Or is the right wish health, the just proportion
Of sun, the acorns and cold pure water, a nest
Out in the country and a place in Rome . . .

Of course, one's aspirations must depend
Upon the opportunities: the justice
That happens to be available; one's fortune.
I think that what the poet meant may be
Something like that; and as for aspiration,
Maybe our aspirations for ourselves
Ought to be different from the hopes we have
(Though there are warnings against too much hope)
When thinking of our children. And in fact
Our fantasies about the perfect life
Are different for ourselves and for our children,
Theirs being safer, less exciting, purer—
And so, depending always on the chances
Our country offers, it seems we should aspire,
For ourselves, to struggle actively to save
The Republic—or to be, if not like Brutus,

Like Quinctius: a citizen of affairs,
Free in the state and in the love of death . . .
While for our children we are bound to aspire
Differently: something like a nest or farm;
So that the cycle of different aspirations
Threads through posterity.
                              And who can say
What Brutus may come sweeping through your
   twenties-
Given the taste you have for noble speeches,
For causes lost and glamourous and just.

Did Horace's father, with his middle-class
And slavish aspirations, have it right?—
To give your child the education fit
For the upper classes: math, philosophy,
And rhetoric in all its branches; so I
Must want for you, when you must fall upon
The sword of government or mortality—
Since all of us, even you, race toward it—to have
The power to make your parting speech in Greek
(Or in the best equivalent) and if
You ever write for fame or money, that Vergil
Will pick your book out from a hundred others,
If that's not plucking at a soldered coin.

Part Three:

Its Everlasting Possibility

I. Braveries

Once, while a famous town lay torn and burning
A woman came to childbed, and lay in labor
While all around her people cursed and screamed
In desperation, and soldiers raged insanely—
So that the child came out, the story says,
In the loud center of every horror of war.
And looking on that scene, just halfway out,
The child retreated backward, to the womb:
And chose to make those quiet walls its urn.

"Brave infant of Saguntum," a poet says—
As though to embrace a limit might show courage.
(Although the word is more like *bravo*, the glory
Of a great tenor, the swagger of new clothes:
The infant as a brilliant moral performer
Defying in its retreat the bounds of life.)

Denial of limit has been the pride, or failing,
Well-known to be shared by all this country's regions,

Races, and classes; which all seem to challenge
The idea of sufficiency itself . . .
And while it seems that in the name of limit
Some people are choosing to have fewer children,
Or none, that too can be a gesture of freedom—
A way to deny or brave the bounds of time.
A boundary is a limit. How can I
Describe for you the boundaries of this place
Where we were born: where Possibility spreads
And multiplies and exhausts itself in growing,
And opens yawning to swallow itself again?
What pictures are there for that limitless grace
Unrealized, horizons ever dissolving?

A field house built of corrugated metal,
The frosted windows tilted open inward
In two lines high along the metal walls;
Inside, a horse-ring and a horse called Yankee
Jogging around the ring with clouds of dust
Rising and settling in the still, cold air
Behind the horse and rider as they course
Rhythmically through the bars of washed-out light
That fall in dim arcades all down the building.

The rider, a girl of seven or eight called Rose,
Concentrates firmly on her art, her body,
Her small, straight back and shoulders as they rise
Together with the alternate, gray shoulders
Of the unweary horse. Her father stands
And watches, in a business suit and coat,
Watching the child's face under the black serge helmet,

Her yellow hair that bounces at her nape
And part-way down her back. He feels the cold
Of the dry, sunless earth up through the soles
Of his thin, inappropriate dress shoes.
He feels the limit of that simple cold,
And braves it, concentrating on the progress
Of the child riding in circles around the ring.
She is so charming that he feels less mortal.
As from the bravery of a fancy suit,
He takes crude courage from the ancient meaning
Of the horse, as from a big car or a business:
He feels as if the world had fewer limits.
The primitive symbols of the horse and girl
Seem goods profound and infinite, as clear
As why the stuffs of merchants are called, "goods."

The goods of all the world seem possible
And clear in that brave spectacle, the rise
Up from the earth and onto the property
Of horses and the history of riding.

In his vague yearning, as he muses on goods
Lost and confused as chivalry, he might
Dream anything: as from the Cavalier
One might dream up the Rodeo, or the Ford,
Or some new thing the country waited for—
Some property, some consuming peasant dream
Of horses and walls; as though the Rodeo
And Ford were elegiac gestures; as though
Invented things gave birth to long-lost goods.

The country, boasting that it cannot see
The past, waits dreaming ever of the past,
Or all the plural pasts: the way a fetus
Dreams vaguely of heaven—waiting, and in its courage
Willing, not only to be born out into
The Actual (with its ambiguous goods),
But to retreat again and be born backward
Into the gallant walls of its potential,
Its sheltered circle ... willing to leave behind,
It might be, carnage.
                              What shall we keep open—
Where shall we throw our courage, where retreat?

White settlers disembarked here, to embark
Upon a mountain-top of huge potential—
Which for the disembarking slaves was low:
A swamp, or valley of dry bones, where they lay
In labor with a brilliant, strange slave-culture—
All emigrants, ever disembarking. *Shall these*
Bones live? And in a jangle of confusion
And hunger, from the mountains to the valleys,
They rise; and breathe; and fall in the wind again.

II. Serpent Knowledge

In something you have written in school, you say
That snakes are born (or hatched) already knowing
Everything they will ever need to know—
Weazened and prematurely shrewd, like Merlin;
Something you read somewhere, I think, some textbook
Coy on the subject of the reptile brain.
(Perhaps the author half-remembered reading
About the Serpent of Experience
That changes manna to gall.) I don't believe it;
Even a snake's horizon must expand,
Inwardly, when an instinct is confirmed
By some new stage of life: to mate, kill, die.

Like angels, who have no genitals or place
Of national origin, however, snakes
Are not historical creatures; unlike chickens,
Who teach their chicks to scratch the dust for food—
Or people, who teach ours how to spell their names:
Not born already knowing all we need,
One generation differing from the next
In what it needs, and knows.

                                        So what I know,
What you know, what your sister knows (approaching
The age you were when I began this poem)
All differ, like different overlapping stretches
Of the same highway: with different lacks, and visions.
The words—"Vietnam"—that I can't use in poems
Without the one word threatening to gape
And swallow and enclose the poem, for you

May grow more finite; able to be touched.
The actual highway—snake's-back where it seems
That any strange thing may be happening, now,
Somewhere along its endless length—once twisted
And straightened, and took us past a vivid place:
Brave in the isolation of its profile,
"Ten miles from nowhere" on the rolling range,
A family graveyard on an Indian mound
Or little elevation above the grassland. . . .
Fenced in against the sky's huge vault at dusk
By a waist-high iron fence with spear-head tips,
The grass around and over the mound like surf.

A mile more down the flat fast road, the homestead:
Regretted, vertical, and unadorned
As its white gravestones on their lonely mound—
Abandoned now, the paneless windows breathing
Easily in the wind, and no more need
For courage to survive the open range
With just the graveyard for a nearest neighbor;
The stones of Limit—comforting and depriving.

Elsewhere along the highway, other limits—
Hanging in shades of neon from dusk to dusk,
The signs of people who know how to take
Pleasure in places where it seems unlikely:
New kinds of places, the "overdeveloped" strips
With their arousing, vacant-minded jumble;
Or garbagey lake-towns, and the tourist-pits
Where crimes unspeakably bizarre come true
To astonish countries older, or more savage . . .

As though the rapes and murders of the French
Or Indonesians were less inventive than ours,
Less goofy than those happenings that grow
Like air-plants—out of nothing, and alone.

They make us parents want to keep our children
Locked up, safe even from the daily papers
That keep the grisly record of that frontier
Where things unspeakable happen along the highways.

In today's paper, you see the teen-aged girl
From down the street; camping in Oregon
At the far point of a trip across the country,
Together with another girl her age,
They suffered and survived a random evil.
An unidentified, youngish man in jeans
Aimed his car off the highway, into the park
And at their tent (apparently at random)
And drove it over them once, and then again;
And then got out, and struck at them with a hatchet
Over and over, while they struggled; until
From fear, or for some other reason, or none,
He stopped; and got back into his car again
And drove off down the night-time highway. No rape,
No robbery, no "motive." Not even words,
Or any sound from him that they remember.
The girl still conscious, by crawling, reached the road
And even some way down it; where some people
Drove by and saw her, and brought them both to help,
So doctors could save them—barely marked.
                                              You see

Our neighbor's picture in the paper: smiling,
A pretty child with a kerchief on her head
Covering where the surgeons had to shave it.
You read the story, and in a peculiar tone—
Factual, not unfeeling, like two policemen—
Discuss it with your sister. You seem to feel
Comforted that it happened far away,
As in a crazy place, in *Oregon:*
For me, a place of wholesome reputation;
For you, a highway where strangers go amok,
As in the universal provincial myth
That sees, in every stranger, a mad attacker . . .
(And in one's victims, it may be, a stranger).

Strangers: the Foreign who, coupling with their cousins
Or with their livestock, or even with wild beasts,
Spawn children with tails, or claws and spotted fur,
Ugly—and though their daughters are beautiful
Seen dancing from the front, behind their backs
Or underneath their garments are the tails
Of reptiles, or teeth of bears.
                                        So one might feel—
Thinking about the people who cross the mountains
And oceans of the earth with separate legends,
To die inside the squalor of sod huts,
Shanties, or tenements; and leave behind
Their legends, or the legend of themselves,
Broken and mended by the generations:
Their alien, orphaned, and disconsolate spooks,
Earth-trolls or Kallikaks or Snopes or golems,

Descended of Hessians, runaway slaves and Indians,
Legends confused and loose on the roads at night . . .
The Alien or Creature of the movies.

As people die, their monsters grow more tame;
So that the people who survived Saguntum,
Or in the towns that saw the Thirty Years' War,
Must have felt that the wash of blood and horror
Changed something, inside. Perhaps they came to see
The state or empire as a kind of Whale
Or Serpent, in whose body they must live—
Not that mere suffering could make us wiser,
Or nobler, but only older, and more ourselves. . . .

On television, I used to see, each week,
Americans descending in machines
With wasted bravery and blood; to spread
Pain and vast fires amid a foreign place,
Among the strangers to whom we were new—
Americans: a spook or golem, there.
I think it made our country older, forever.
I don't mean better or not better, but merely
As though a person should come to a certain place
And have his hair turn gray, that very night.
Someday, the War in Southeast Asia, somewhere—
Perhaps for you and people younger than you—
Will be the kind of history and pain
Saguntum is for me; but never tamed
Or "history" for me, I think. I think
That I may always feel as if I lived
In a time when the country aged itself:

More lonely together in our common strangeness . . .
As if we were a family, and some members
Had done an awful thing on a road at night,
And all of us had grown white hair, or tails:
And though the tails or white hair would afflict
Only that generation then alive
And of a certain age, regardless whether
They were the ones that did or planned the thing—
Or even heard about it—nevertheless
The members of that family ever after
Would bear some consequence or demarcation,
Forgotten maybe, taken for granted, a trait,
A new syllable buried in their name.

III. Mysteries of the Future

People stream slowly from a city church,
Their clothes bright in the sudden winter daylight,
Their bodies clean and warm inside the cloth
Like flags and armor in the dazzling air,
Sun flashing and wincing from the curbside ice.
Their pace is dreamy, strolling to their cars
Over the gritty sidewalk, in Sunday clothes.

It is Chicago; and though in many ways
It could be some place in another country,
The way I see the people and the church—
As mysteries, not just unknown or foreign—
Makes it this country: and Chicago, a setting
We make as we discover. It makes me think
Of how small children, with laborious
And grubby fingers, improvise a scene
From disproportionate, inspired arrangements
Of toys and objects: mirror for a pond,
And gathered on the shore amid strange buildings,
In mad, pedantic order, animals
And people. The squirrel, immense, bears on his
    shoulders
Riders including an anthropomorphic lion,
In pants and glasses. Barnyard and jungle creatures
Have landed their airplane—some are on the wings—
Right on the hotel roof. Wagons and cars
Parade down to the water. . . .

                                    The girls and women
In pretty colors, the males in blue or brown,

Pause eddying on the steps, as though to blink
Like science-fiction travelers through time,
Uncertain if the surfaces they see
So brazenly gleaming mean to hail them toward
The mysteries of the past, or of the future.

Whether they have slept in church or not, they look
Refreshed in spirit, ready for the cuisine
And music of this era ahead or back,
Younger or older than the one they knew.

"For here we have no continuing city, but seek
For one to come"—*Hebrews*, 13: 14.
I can't say if our country is old, or young.
The future is an electrocuting thought—
That stuns the thinking reed to quiet, and heightens
The sense that everything we make is mortal,
Or part of some continuing epitaph.
Our very sentences are like a cloth
Cut shimmering from conventions of the dead—
Hung sometimes to flutter from a spar or gallant,
Nudged forward like the paper boats of candy
Launched for the gods downriver, in the future.

If I could sail forward to see the streets
Of that strange country where you will live past me,
Or further even by a hundred years;
And walk those pavements with my phantom steps,
And find Chicago flashing in winter sun;
And church doors ready to swing open, or melt
Before my penetrating ghost—my courage

Would fail, I think: best not to mount the steps
Where I could leave no footprint in the snow . . .
Best not to see those garments.

                                          The shining casket,
Pure gold, where Philip of Macedonia lay
Twenty-three hundred years, and his breastplate
And greaves of gold and ivory, are gorgeous still;
But all the treasury of woven fabrics
And splendid leather that lay around the king
Technicians using instruments can deduce
Only from the fine dust scattered on the floor
Around the casket; the long hardwood handle
Of his bright spear fell slowly to a powder
Where it was propped, and left the point adhering
Eerily to the stonework of the wall.

It's fearful to leave anything behind,
To choose or make some one thing to survive
Into the future—where the air and light
That spread around us here in all directions
Stand ready to dim, discolor, and unravel
The colors that we fit around our bodies,
Precious and mutable, a second skin.
(Although the soul may be immortal, or not—
And some believe that even the body may rise—
Our cloth must die, and parch away forever.)

Jefferson in his epitaph records
That he was author of the Declaration
Of Independence, and of the Virginia law
Providing public education; and founder

Of that state's University—omitting
His "high office" . . . as if it were a bound,
Or something held, not something he had done—
The ceremonial garment he had been given
By others, with a certain solemn function
And honor; eventually, to be removed.

The church, Gothic Revival, and waiting cars
With brightwork glinting through a haze of salt
Suggest Nostalgia and Progress—which are in spirit
Less blatant, intimate, tragic than Epitaph:
As though the people, blood rising to their cheeks
As they walk into the cold, could leave behind
The image of themselves in their good clothes—
To survive as a memorial, compacted
By twenty centuries of the slowest fire
As if to something made of stone, or metal.

In the familiar boast or accusation
Americans have scant "historic sense";
Nostalgia and Progress seem to be our frail
National gestures against the enveloping,
Suffusive nightmare of time—which swallows first
The unaware, because they are least free . . .
But time's nightmare, and freedom from it, differ
For different peoples: like their burial customs;
And what they choose to say in what they leave.
To speak words few enough to fit a stone,
And frame them as if speaking from the past
Into the void or mystery of the future,
Demands that we be naked, free, and final:

God wills us free, man wills us slaves.
I will as God wills Gods will be done.
Here lies the body of
JOHN JACK
A native of Africa who died
MARCH 1773 aged about 60 years

Tho' born in a land of slavery,
He was born free,
Tho' he lived in a land of liberty,
He lived a slave,
Till by his honest, tho' stolen labors,
He acquired the source of slavery,
Which gave him his freedom,
Tho' not long before
Death the Grand Tyrant
Gave him his final emancipation,
And set him on a footing with kings.
Tho' a slave to vice,
He practiced those virtues
Without which kings are but slaves.

IV. Epilogue: Endings

"Pregnant again with the old twins, Hope and Fear"
I'll write you one more time. You're older now,
By three years. And when the college students do
The Winter's Tale, you're charming as Mammilius,
The small bold Prince who starts what seems to be
A story about a ghost, and dies offstage
Before Act III is over—in time for bedtime,
Though you prefer to stay through each rehearsal,
As pleased as Puck, among the all-girl cast:
A kind of Court of Ladies, and you a page
Or favorite, a dwarf in jeans like theirs,
One of the group, all business, though inwardly
Half-drunk on glamour.
                 "Looking on the lines
Of my boy's face," the girl who plays your father
Pronounces, in lines you say from memory
As I drive you to rehearsal, "I did recoil
Twenty-three years, and saw myself unbreeched,
In my green velvet coat; my dagger muzzled,
Lest it should bite its master, and so prove,
As ornaments oft do, too dangerous."

Children are dangerous hostages to fortune—
Though they may seem, as to that fallible king,
Ornaments to our sentimental past,
They bind us to the future: Hope and Fear;
And though we might recoil, they make us strain
To see the wintry desert out beyond us.

On Opening Night, in hose and velvet tunic,
You say, "a sad tale's best for winter"—and yet,
The ending is happy; though the Bear eats the man,
Though the pastoral is broken, and the King alone
Upon the wind-scarred peak of his regret,
It all comes right: the statue comes to life,
And frozen Possibility moves and breathes,
Refreshed again, although the King is older.
Though happy endings rarely satisfy,
That one's a model of successful failure,
Holding Truth up against the rules of Romance.

The repetitious Phoenix, on her nest
Of burning contradictions, affronts belief
Like some impossible happy ending, as though
The country were just a dream—a pastoral
Delusion of the dirt and rocks and trees,
Or daydream of Leviathan himself,
A Romance of implausible rebirths.

The mountains intimate a different kind
Of ending: a cold and motionless remove.
High up above the treeline the clear dry air
Even in the warmest August noon conveys
A hint of snow; a crystal needle tickles
The nostrils a little, even while the eyes
Water and squint against the gray rock flashing,
The brightness of the sky.
                              In the Sierras,
Where Winter's never far, the country is clear,
A stage of granite swept for meditation—

Irrelevant to the saunas, Volkswagens and woks
As British mountains are to tea and curry,
The exotic and assimilated clutter
Of treasure that expansion washed ashore.
Up there, a miner or drifter might expand
Upon his solitude and drift away
Over the ridges deep in muffling snow,
Feel free from all the clutter of hopes and fears,
And let his breath diffuse in the lucid cold.

Nothing can seem more final than the mountains,
Where Empires seem to grow and fade like moss—
But even mountains have come to need protection,
By special laws and organized committees,
From our ingenuities, optimism, needs.
The passion to make new beginnings can shatter
The highest solitude, or living rock. . . .

One might end with disgust for such renewals:
The old bear lumbers from the hibernation
Of all his crimes and losses; the new sunlight,
Resurgent, falls in a halo on his grizzle,
And he feels young again—*America,*
The air that serves me with the breath to speak . . .
In the "Minnesota Belt" from Times Square west
For five blocks, children, boy and girl blonde hustlers
Imported from the Midwest, haunt all night—
Just as young children were sold in the Haymarket
Of William Morris's London, or the bazaars
Of ancient, drowsy Empires. But "It avails not,
Time nor place, distance avails not"; the country shrugs,

It is a cruel young profile from a coin,
Innocent and immortal in the religion
Of its own founding, and whatever happens
In actual New York, it is not final,
But a mere episode . . . and on some stage
As bare and rarefied as the coldest mountain,
With an authority transcending power
Or even belief, New Hope is born again,
And though it demand an Aztec vivisection
Everything lost must be made whole again.

A sad tale's best for winter, but the country
Sprawls over several zones of time and climate,
Never with any one season: the year itself
In no fixed place. Where nothing will stand still
Nothing can end—but recoils into the past,
Or is improvised into the dream or nightmare
Romance of new beginnings.
                              On a lake
Beyond the fastness of a mountain pass
The Asian settlers built a dazzling city
Of terraced fountains and mosaic walls,
With rainbow-colored carp and garish birds
To adorn the public gardens. In the streets,
The artisans of feathers, bark or silk
Traded with trappers, with French and Spanish priests
And Scottish grocers. From the distant peaks,
The fabulous creatures of the past descended
To barter or to take wives: minotaur
And centaur clattered on the cobbled streets

With Norseman and Gipsy; from the ocean floor
The mermaid courtesans came to Baltimore,
New Orleans, Galveston, their gilded aquaria
Tended by powdered Blacks. Nothing was lost—
Or rather, nothing seemed to begin or end
In ways they could remember. The Founders made
A Union mystic yet rational, and sudden,
As if suckled by the very wolf of Rome . . .
Indentured paupers and criminals grew rich
Trading tobacco; molasses; cotton; and slaves
With names like horses, or from Scott or Plutarch.
In the mills, there was every kind of name,
With even "Yankee" a kind of *jankel* or Dutchman.
The Yankees pulled stones from the earth, to farm,
And when the glacial boulders were piled high,
Skilled masons came from Parma and Piacenza
And settled on Division Street and Oak Street
And on the narrow side streets between them. In winter,
Mr. Diehl hired Italian boys to help
Harvest the ice from Diehl's Pond onto sledges
And pack it into icehouses, where it kept
To be cut and delivered all summer long.
The Linden Apartments stand where Diehl's Pond was;
But even when I was little, the iceman came
To houses that had iceboxes, and we could beg
Splinters to suck, or maybe even a ride,
Sitting on wet floorboards and steaming tarps
As far as Saint Andrew's, or the V.F.W.
The Eagles, Elks, Moose, Masons each had a building:
I pictured them like illustrations from *Alice.*

As television came in, the lodges faded,
But people began to group together by hobbies,
Each hobby with its magazines and clubs;
My father still played baseball twice a week;
And even after you were born, the schools
And colleges were places set apart,
As of another time; and one time you
Performed in *The Winter's Tale*.

                        And at the end,
As people applauded louder and louder, you
Stood with young girls who wore gray wigs and beards,
All smiling and holding hands—as if the Tale
Had not been sad at all, or was all a dream,
And winter was elsewhere, howling on the mountains
Unthinkably old and huge and far away—
At the far opposite edge of our whole country,
So large, and strangely broken, and unforeseen.

MEMORIAL

(J.E. AND N.M.S.)

Here lies a man. And here, a girl. They live
In the kind of artificial life we give

To birds or statues: imagining what they feel,
Or that like birds the dead each had one call,

Repeated, or a gesture that suspends
Their being in a forehead or the hands.

A man comes whistling from a house. The screen
Snaps shut behind him. Though there is no man

And no house, memory sends him to get tools
From a familiar shed, and so he strolls

Through summer shade to work on the family car.
He is my uncle, and fresh home from the war,

With little for me to remember him doing yet.
The clock of the cancer ticks in his body, or not,

Depending if it is there, or waits. The search
Of memory gains and fails like surf: the porch

And trim are painted cream, the shakes are stained.
The shadows could be painted (so little wind

Is blowing there) or stains on the crazy-paving
Of the front walk. . . . Or now, the shadows are moving:

Another house, unrelated; a woman says,
Is this your special boy, and the girl says, yes,

Moving her hand in mine. The clock in her, too—
As someone told me a month or two ago,

Months after it finally took her. A public building
Is where the house was: though a surf, unyielding

And sickly, seethes and eddies at the stones
Of the foundation. The dead are made of bronze,

But dying they were like birds with clocklike hearts—
Unthinkable, how much pain the tiny parts

Of even the smallest bird might yet contain.
We become larger than life in how much pain

Our bodies may encompass . . . all Titans in that,
Or heroic statues. Although there is no heat

Brimming in the fixed, memorial summer, the brows
Of lucid metal sweat a faint warm haze

As I try to think the pain I never saw.
Though there is no pain there, the small birds draw

Together in crowds above the houses—and cry
Over the surf: as if there were a day,

Memorial, marked on the calendar for dread
And pain and loss—although among the dead

Are no hurts, but only emblematic things;
No hospital beds, but a lifting of metal wings.

GPSR Authorized Representative: Easy Access System Europe - Mustamäe tee
50, 10621 Tallinn, Estonia, gpsr.requests@easproject.com